Copyright © 2016 by Lani Sharp
All rights reserved. This book or any portion thereof
may not be reproduced or used in any manner whatsoever
without the express written permission of the publisher
except for the use of brief quotations in a book review.

Printed in Australia

First Printing, 2016

ISBN: 978-0-9945051-3-2

White Light Publishing House
6 Lincoln Way
Melton West, VIC, Australia 3337

www.whitelightpublishingau.com

✥ DEDICATIONS ✥

This book is wholly dedicated to my beautiful daughter Allira, the most inspiring, wonderful, loving, and amazing Cancerian in my Universe. Words can't express my love for your precious heart and soul. I love you to the Moon and back, my special girl.

ABOUT THE AUTHOR

☾ ★ ☽

Lani Sharp is a Natural Born Rebel who just also happens to be an Aquarian, who shunned 'conventional' astrology courses to pursue her own path in the wondrous, inspiring and ever-evolving field of cosmic forces and stellar influences. After failing to find a course or tutor that suited her needs, Lani set out on her own starry Magic Carpet adventure across the skies, partly to discover her own 'truths' about this ancient system, but mostly to prove that one can achieve absolutely anything, including and above all, their dream careers (or lifestyle), if they put their hearts and souls into it. A self-taught astrologer who takes the esoteric and spiritual approach to this much-loved popular art, she has been studying and effectively practising astrology since she was eight years old. When she is not writing about, channelling, practising or teaching astrology, she can be found living her dream life alternating somewhere between her home in Australia's stunning Tropical North or her second home in Victoria's beautiful Dandenong Ranges, enjoying tea parties with her highly imaginative Cancerian daughter, Allira, and their gnome and fairy friends, crystal-wishing, day-dreaming, believing in gnomes, pixies, angels, fairies, magic and miracles, honing her magickal * witchcraft skills, Moon-gazing, Sun-worshipping, Venus-channelling, Jupiter-drawing, assisting others to discover, unravel and follow their true spiritual paths … or of course walking across rainbows!

Not a mistake. Magick is a Wiccan variation of the word 'magic'.

★

ACKNOWLEDGEMENTS, CREDITS & GRATITUDE BLESSINGS

✯

I would love to thank the following people and entities for their amazing contributions, interest, support and faith in me as I wrote the manuscripts for each of the twelve astrological Sun signs. Firstly, the biggest thank you go to my Mum, Sandra, and my stepdad, Barry, for their unending support, love, advice, daily Skype conversations, acceptance of our geographical distance, and above all, their inner knowing that everything always comes together in the end. Your support of me and my dreams is appreciated beyond words. Secondly, gratitude to my wonderful partner, Travis, for his patience (no mean feat for a Gemini!), for supporting me every step of the way, and for his acceptance of my 'mad scientist' Aquarian mindset by never trying to break down the invisible 'laboratory' walls I built around myself while writing the books. I would also like to extend my enormous gratitude to the following: Allira, my little Cancerian 'crab' daughter, a soul in a billion, who also had to tolerate and operate within the bounds of her nutty professor mother's antics and focus throughout the writing of the books. Thank you to Nicola, my wonderful Facebook friend, for recommending White Light Publishing House, and of course to White Light Publishing House themselves, for pouring their faith and passion into my project from the very beginning - and an even bigger thank you to the wonderful people behind the company for publishing my work, Christie and Jess! Gratitude also goes out to my dear friends, both near and far, who have inspired in me so many ideas through simply being themselves - especially Amanda and Carlie. Amanda, you have always been my 'astrology buddy' and I have always enjoyed - and learned so much through - our discussions on all things astrology and star signs: the good, the bad and the ugly! Having someone like you off which to bounce thoughts and share ideas with, has always been immensely helpful and appreciated. I have saved my final thank you for The Universe, who always delivers to me exactly what I have asked for, without exception. The Universe is my ultimate *higher power*, my guiding light, my powerful driving force, my spiritual helper, my guardian angel, my eternal friend, my inner motivator, my sympathetic listener, my inspirational teacher, and the fulfiller of all my dreams, including this one, having my very first book(s) published, a long-held dream that stretches way back through the years to my days of being a mini dreamer, inquisitor and stargazer. The Universe has always believed in me, but perhaps more importantly, I have always believed in *IT*.

So to all of the above, I wish to say:

Thank you, thank you, thank you!

"There was a star danced,
and under that I was born"

William Shakespeare

"We were born at a given moment, in a given place, and like vintage years of wine, we have the qualities of the year and of the season in which we are born"

Carl G. Jung

INSPIRED BY ALL THE SIGNS

Aries imparted courage and boldness
And helped me dance away the pain
Taurus gave me hugs and comfort
And shelter from the rain
Gemini provided me with laughter
And taught me again how to have fun
Cancer nurtured and sustained me
By reflecting back my Sun
Leo reminded me there was joy
From within myself and above
Virgo awakened my healthy glow
By teaching me how to love
Libra gave me gentle hugs
And judged me not for a thing
Scorpio lent me some of his power
And took away the sting
Sagittarius showered me with gifts
Of words so wise and true
As Capricorn led the way up the mountain
My resolve and strength grew
Aquarius gave me the gift of friendship
And carried me as his brother
And Pisces swam with me to the depths
With a compassion like no other.

Special Note

Throughout the text of this book, and indeed the whole Lucky Astrology book series, I have capitalised the first letter of the word 'Universe'. This is because, quite simply, I feel it is a very special title for the higher power that I personally choose to be guided by, and have accordingly highlighted it as such.

You may also notice that I use the words 'he' or 'she', and 'his' or 'her', when referring to your own Sun sign and other zodiac signs, and never 'he or she' or 'his or her' together. The reason for this is for simplicity, for I don't wish the sentences to be too wordy and therefore the messages within them to be lost. As a general rule, I refer to all six 'masculine' zodiac signs as 'he', and all six 'feminine' signs as 'she', and this remains a consistent rule throughout this book and the whole series.

Your Sun sign, Cancer, is a feminine sign and will thus be referred to accordingly.

CONTENTS

	Page
ASTROLOGY	15
THE ZODIAC AND YOUR PLACE IN THE SUN	24
CANCER THE CRAB	31
QUOTES BY CANCERIANS	38
THE CANCER CONSTELLATION	43
THE CANCERIAN SYMBOL	45
THE RUNDOWN ★ THE ESSENCE OF CANCER	48
THE THREE DECANS OF CANCER	63
YOUR ELEMENT ★ WATER	67
YOUR MODE ★ CARDINAL	91
YOUR RULING PLANET ★ THE MOON	93
YOUR HOUSE IN THE HOROSCOPE ★ THE FOURTH HOUSE	109
YOUR OPPOSITE SIGN ★ CAPRICORN	114
MAGIC, DRAWING, ATTRACTION, SPELLS, RITUALS, WISHING & POWER	124
ASTROLOGY & MAGIC	129
PLANETS ★ DAYS OF THE WEEK & THEIR POWERS	135
YOUR NATAL MOON PHASE	139
SPELLS, MAGIC & WISHING WITH MOON PHASES	142
THE MOON IN THE HUMAN PSYCHE & NATAL CHART	150
YOUR MOON SIGN	153
YOUR BODY & HEALTH	161
THE CELL SALTS ★ ASTROLOGICAL TONICS	167

	Page
WATER SIGN CANCER & THE PHLEGMATIC HUMOUR	170
MONEY ATTRIBUTES	173
COLOURS ★ YOUR LUCKY COLOURS	176
LUCKY CAREER TIPS	189
LUCKY PLACES	193
GEMS & CRYSTALS	194
CANCERIAN POWER CRYSTALS	205
YOUR LUCKY NUMBERS	216
YOUR LUCKY MAGIC HOURS OR TIME UNITS	224
YOUR LUCKY DAY ★ MONDAY	229
YOUR LUCKY CHARM / TALISMANS	233
YOUR LUCKY ANIMALS & BIRDS	235
YOUR METALS	252
PLANTS, HERBS, SPICES, TREES, SHRUBS, FLOWERS, SCENTS & INCENSE	255
YOUR FOODS	261
YOUR LUCKY WOOD & CELTIC TREE ★ BIRCH & OAK OR HOLLY	263
THE POWER OF LOVE	272
LUCKY IN LOVE? CANCER COMPATIBILITY	284
YOUR TAROT CARDS	300
LUCKY 13 TIPS	314
HAVE YOU PACKED YOUR MAGICAL BAG FOR THE JOURNEY?	317
A FINAL WORD ★ TAPPING INTO THE MAGIC OF CANCER	318

LUCKY ASTROLOGY

By Lani Sharp

CANCER

Tapping into the Powers of Your Sun Sign for Greater Luck, Happiness, Health, Abundance & Love

"That which is above is like to that which is below, and that which is below is like to that which is above, to accomplish the miracles of one thing ... the Father thereof is the Sun, the mother the Moon."

The Emerald Tablet, Hermes Trismegistus (circa 3000 BC)

★ ASTROLOGY ★

Astrology: "Divination through the correlation of earthly events with celestial patterns"
'Real Magic', I. Bonewits, 1971

A BRIEF HISTORY

Astrology can be defined as the calculation and meaningful interpretation of the positions and motions of the heavenly bodies, and their correlation with human experiences. Its central concept is based upon this interconnectedness or correspondence between the stars and ourselves.

The word astrology is derived from the Greek word astron, meaning 'star' and logos which means 'word'. Astrology, therefore, literally means language of the stars. It is based on the ancient law known as 'As Above, So Below', otherwise known as the Law of the Macrocosm and Microcosm. The Macrocosm is the Universe, symbolised by the sky, the starry dome that we can see from the Earth; the Microcosm is us - humans, and all other life on Earth. 'As Above, So Below' is a well-known and deeply impressing maxim of Hermetic origin, inscribed upon the famed Emerald Tablet among cryptic wording by enigmatic figure, Hermes Trismegistus, around 5,000 years ago. These four powerful words are adopted by astrologers and believers in magic to explain, in very succinct wording, the meaning behind the art and science of celestial influences upon our Earthly affairs.

Astrology and many other magical and occult studies, propose that we are not separate from the Universe, we are part of it. The Sun, Moon and planets all follow exact patterns of movement and their motions can be measured precisely by astronomers. The basic idea of astrology is that all individual parts of the Universe, from plants to animals, cooperate with each other and work together in harmony.

Anyone can apply astrological knowledge in their daily lives, but it hasn't always been like that. At one time, astrology was reserved only for Kings and nations, and only the court astrologer/astronomer could cast and interpret horoscopes. Ancient astrology and astronomy used to be one and the same. To be an astrologer, you first had to be able to interpret the stars in some systematic way, and then track the movement of the Moon and the planets against the background of the constellations.

Astrology, the knowledge and language of the cosmos, goes back to the ancient kingdom of Babylonia and was adapted by the Mesopotamians, Greeks, Egyptians and Romans to incorporate their own deities (as indicated in mythology). It is upon a combination of Greek and Egyptian interpretations of astrology that our present knowledge is based.

In the ancient Mesopotamian world, as far back as 800 BC, people lived precariously beneath the open skies. The skies and the stars which filled them, were the real founders of astrology. Today we are aware that the Sun and Moon exert a profound influence upon our Earthly affairs, but for our primitive ancestors, the heavens, the stars and the planets must have been a matter of great and mysterious significance. Early humankind, its senses influenced by natural processes of ebbs, flows, growth, decay and cycles, tended naturally towards a physical explanation of the Universe. At first, the movements of the planets - and all celestial occurrences - were observed as omens affecting the Ruler and his nation; it was only in Egypt in the fifth century AD that the casting of horoscopes for individual people and the calculation of the planetary positions at the time of birth became widespread.

The first astrologers, the Chaldeans, mapped the stars and later passed this knowledge and wisdom on to the ancient Greeks, who, during the third century BC, developed astrology into a science with the use of mathematical aids and instruments to measure planetary movements. The Greeks were the first to cast individual horoscopes. And it was the Greeks who associated the four elements with the signs of the zodiac. The word "zodiac" can be translated from Greek to mean the "circle or path of the animals." The Greeks not only had names for the twelve Solar phases but had symbols for each, and many correspond with the ones we use today.

The Greeks passed on much of their knowledge to the Romans. During the second century BC, Roman astrologers were primarily forecasters who were consulted frequently by rulers of the church and state. By the early third century AD, astrology co-existed with early Christianity. This harmonious co-existence was possible because it was considered that celestial bodies could foretell events, but did not determine the future - indeed, the stars seen by the shepherds at the time of Christ's birth were only predictors of his arrival. After the fourth century AD, Christianity strengthened and the popularity of astrology declined as Christian reluctance to support 'pagan' or 'superstitious' beliefs became more prominent. The Middle Ages saw a revival in astrology, with courses being taught in universities and other educational establishments, and connections were made between the zodiac, alchemy, herbs and medicine. Astrology was once again able to exist alongside the Church, although many remained suspicious of astrologers.

Around the beginning of the fifteenth century, academics of the Renaissance movement examined the past for knowledge, and ancient philosophies, including astrology, flourished; this coincided with arts and science movements developing. The famous prophet and astrologer Nostradamus lived during this period. Leonardo da Vinci depicted aspects of astrology combined with geometry in his art. Writers and poets of the time, including Shakespeare, alluded to zodiacal influences in their work.

During this period, astrology had numerous practical applications. Agricultural calendars were introduced, indicating favourable planting times according to the phases of the Moon; health and illness were linked with movements of celestial bodies; and emotional states and mental health afflictions correlated with the planetary positions.

Eventually, new ways of thinking led to a split between astronomy and astrology, and by the seventeenth century, the realm of science had developed to such a degree that astrology was no longer taken seriously.

The study of the sky above us has been charted for more than 5,000 years. This fact is known because ancient 'horoscopes' imprinted on clay tablets have been unearthed, dating back almost 5,400 years ago. However, no one knows for certain just how, when and where astrology first began, although it is known that it flourished in ancient Chaldea, Mesopotamia, Babylon and Egypt.

Astrology is a science which has spanned many centuries and still remains extraordinarily popular, and its truths have the potential to speak to and *through* all of us. Long before today's interest in it, men of great vision such as Ptolemy, Hippocrates, Plato, Galileo, Jefferson, Franklin, Newton, Columbus and Jung respected its inherent truths, mythology and eternal knowledge. Furthermore, astrology predates many other 'sciences' - for out of it grew religion, medicine and astronomy, not the other way around.

The discipline of astrology is ultimately a study of the interlocking and interrelated forces of the twelve zodiacal forces, or constellations, that grace the heavens, as they pour their energies into the Earthly kingdoms below. As these various energies circulate throughout the etheric realm of our Solar system, these zodiacal entities and archetypes imprint their vibrational frequencies and harmonic resonances upon our bodies, minds, souls and spirits.

ASTROLOGY & THE INDIVIDUAL

Since the earliest period of the history of humankind, people studied the starry vaults of the heavens and conceived that their presence, movements and positions endowed planet Earth's inhabitants with Divine influence. There is much evidence that positions and movements of the planets as seen from Earth at the time of a birth are linked to personality characteristics of individuals. Human energy and emotional cycles are governed by the forces and networks of magnetic impulses from all the planets. Of all the heavenly bodies, the Moon's effects and power are the most marked and visible due to its close proximity to Earth. But the Sun, Venus, Mars, Mercury, Jupiter, Saturn, Uranus, Neptune and Pluto exercise their influences just as surely. In fact, scientists are aware that plants and animals are affected by natural cycles which are governed by forces such as fluctuations in barometric pressure, the gravitational field and electricity in the air. These Earthly dynamics are originally triggered by magnetic vibrations from the atmosphere, or outer space, from where the planets send forth their unseen waves. No living organism or mineral on Earth escapes these immense, if unseen, influences.

The geomagnetic field seems to affect life on Earth in certain observed ways, and these influences appear to correlate with planetary positions. It has been suggested that the fluctuations of the Earth's magnetic field are picked up by the nervous system of the in utero infant, which acts like an antenna, and these synchronise the internal biological clocks of the foetus which control the moment of birth. The foetal magnetic antenna therefore, is sensitive enough to sense these planetary vibrations and fields, and through a combination of inherited genetics and the positions of the planets at birth, they are imprinted with certain basic inherited and 'absorbed' personality characteristics.

Carl Jung, the Swiss psychiatrist and psychological theorist, suggested that the inherent disposition of the individual is present at birth, and is reflected in the patterns of his or her natal chart. Further, he theorised that there is a 'priori factor' in all human activities, namely the inborn, preconscious and unconscious individual structure of the psyche. The preconscious psyche, for example that of a newborn baby, is not simply an empty vessel into which practically anything can be poured, but rather it is this preconscious psyche that gives us the free will to become what we are instead of what others or our environment makes us. The child is not merely a receptacle for the psychic life of those around him or her, albeit sensitive and susceptible to the surrounding unconscious forces in childhood; for he/she also brings something of his own to his experience of them.

Further, Dr Harold S. Burr, who was a Professor of Anatomy at the Yale University School of Medicine, and author of *The Nature of Man and the Meaning of Existence* (1962), asserted that there is order in the Universe, unity in the organism and man is endowed with a soul. He stated that a complex magnetic field not only establishes the pattern of the human brain at birth, but continues to regulate and control it through life, and that the human central nervous system is a superb receptor of electro-magnetic energies, indeed the finest in nature. He contended that the electro-dynamic fields of all living things, which may be measured and mapped with standard voltmeters, mould and control each organism's development, health and mood, and named these fields 'fields of life'.

It can therefore be suggested that astrological and planetary influences endow us with the majority of our characteristics at birth, characteristics bestowed upon us according to our Sun sign and other planetary forces. Other parts of the chart are also highly significant and need to be integrated for a 'whole' picture to form, however the Sun sign is an excellent starting point.

The ancients taught that astrology was one of the keys to the many enigmas that plague humans in their unceasing quest to determine what the meaning of life is, and what their role and place in the Universe is - and this quest still persists today. Astrology, which dates back over 5,000 years, is indeed one such key to unlocking the many secrets of the Universe - and ultimately, the individual self.

"KNOW THYSELF"

"Man, know thyself.
All wisdom centres on this."
Carl Jung

Before the temple of the Oracle at Delphi, the ancient Greeks imparted a special piece of advice that was carved onto one of the portals: "Know Thyself." These two powerful words are easy enough to understand, but much more difficult to apply. Throughout life's inner and outer journey, astrology can provide us with an inner navigational system by which we can be guided towards our highest potential, and closer towards the eternal quest of 'knowing thyself'. It provides the hope that this higher spiritual plane exists and that if we can 'read' and therefore be guided by the unique inner blueprint that our individual birth chart has stamped upon us at the moment we take our very first breath, indeed we can reach this higher spiritual plane and realise our innate potential.

Always remember that astrology is not fatalistic. The stars may incline, but they do not compel. Astrology simply provides us with an inner guide, a blueprint, for our journey through life and the finding of our true selves - and what we do with the resulting knowledge is entirely up to us.

Good luck on your journey!

THE ZODIAC & YOUR PLACE IN THE SUN

The zodiac is a circle of 360 degrees, consisting of equal segments of 30 degrees each. These represent the twelve houses of the twelve astrological signs. This zodiac is how the early astrologers imagined the Solar system to be, a perfect circle with the Earth at its centre, around which the Sun, Moon and the planets revolved. Each sign of the zodiac corresponds to one of the twelve segments, following a chronological order and established according to the rhythm of the seasons and cycles of the Sun and the Moon. But the zodiac itself, or the band of constellations which comprise it, has shifted over the millennia, creating division between astronomical and astrological schools of thought. It has been said that due to this shift over time, one who once considered themselves as an Aquarian, is actually a Capricorn, the sign before it, and a Leo is actually a Cancerian, its preceding sign. This is the result of misunderstandings and differences in perspectives, and explanations around it are beyond the scope of this book, but can be researched further should you wish to delve a little deeper.

From the astronomical point of view, it is true that the zodiac to which we refer today is not situated where it 'should' be, but indeed, nothing is fixed under the celestial vault. And so the starting point of the ancient zodiac does not correspond exactly to the one we can observe today. But for the purposes of increasing your power and luck, let's keep things simple and enjoy the ride; after all, astrology - while based upon many scientific theories, mysteries, scepticism, superstitions, facts, measurable patterns, ambiguities, correlations, paradoxes, contradictions, links, stigmatisms and observations that seek to support, refute, prove and disprove this ancient art time and again - is ultimately meant to be *fun* too!

THE SUN

Earth's Luminary ★ *Our Brightest Shining Star*

Our Centre, Core Self, Identity & Inner Guiding Light

"Perfect is what I have said of the work of the Sun."
Hermes Trismegistus, *The* Emerald *Tablet*

The Sun is our essence, centre, source, ego strength, power, life force, will, vitality, creative expression, purpose, life's direction, our sense of identity, and who we really *are*. Our brightest star is the core of our individuality, our inner guiding light. The Sun is externalising, and represents totality, infinity, eternity, the striving toward and ultimate reaching of one's personal destiny, and *completion* in all areas. It is the creative energising giver of life and the 'father' of the zodiac. It endows us with our inherent creative potential and personal identity - our urge to *create* and to *be*. The Sun is our core self, conscious purpose, our sense of creating something out of our own being. It is the integrated personality and represents the *present*, our greatest Gift. The Sun rules the heart and is thus symbolically the centre of self. Indeed, the Sun *is* the heart and the most commanding presence in our birth chart; the luminary Ruler who governs our essential self and wants to be noticed and appreciated, and above all, to *shine*.

★ KEY WORDS ★

Identity, core self, spirit, life force, power, essence, creativity, higher self, the Father, ego, vitality, pride, individuality, leadership, majesty, inner authority, will, expression, willpower, purpose, the journey, the path and the destiny.

THE SUN ★ THE ULTIMATE SOURCE OF LIFE ON EARTH

Throughout the ages, and indeed since life forms began, the electromagnetic waves generated by the Sun have kept planet Earth habitable for humans, animals, plants and minerals. The Sun is, in fact, the only true source of energy on planet Earth. It provides the perfect amount of energy for plants to synthesise all of the products required for growth and reproduction, which is then stored by plants and ingested by humans and animals who, through many complex processes, utilise these various forms of encapsulated Solar energy - and so the cycle continues. Wood, fuel and minerals (crystals included), too, are merely various forms of this encased Sun energy. In fact all matter is essentially 'frozen' light. Human body cells are bundles of Sun energy; we couldn't conceive or process a single thought without the molecules of Solar-energised oxygen and glucose.

In essence, the Sun supports the growth of all species, including human beings and microscopic life forms, and without it life on Earth would simply not be possible. The mathematical and metaphysical complexity that stands behind a system of organisation and order so infinitely diverse and intricate as planetary life cannot be truly fathomed, but unerringly and miraculously, the Sun instinctively knows what each species, from a tree to a human, intrinsically needs in order to fulfil its evolutionary purpose and cycles.

Ultimately, the electromagnetic waves generated by the Sun come in a variety of lengths, which determine their specific course of action and responsibility. There are gamma rays, x-rays, cosmic rays, various kinds of ultraviolet rays, infrared, short-wave infrared, radio waves, electric waves, and of course the visible light spectrum, consisting of the seven colour rays.

Most of these energy waves are absorbed and used for various processes in the layers of atmosphere that encircle the Earth, and only a small portion of them - the electromagnetic spectrum - reach the surface of our planet. Although the human eye is only able to perceive about one percent of this spectrum, the waves exert a very strong influence upon us. The waves and rays which do affect us so profoundly, allow all life forms to undergo constant cycles of change necessary for growth and renewal. Physically, we can observe this, but on a deeper, more spiritual plane, we can even *feel* it and allow its radiance to permeate our very souls. Such is the might, force and power of that astonishing ball of fire in our sky: the brilliant, ever-shining Sun.

THE SUN ★ WHAT IT REPRESENTS IN THE HUMAN PSYCHE & NATAL CHART

☼

"The Sun is the most powerful of all the stellar bodies. It colours the personality so strongly that an amazingly accurate picture can be given of the individual who was born when it was exercising its power through the known and predicable influences of a certain astrological sign; these electromagnetic vibrations will continue to stamp that person with the characteristics of their Sun sign as they go through life."
***Linda Goodman's Sun Signs*, Linda Goodman, Pan Books, 1968**

The Sun is our essence, our core self, conscious purpose and sense of identity, our creative potential, our spirit, the integrated personality that shines outward from within us. It is concerned with the present. It is our centre, source, power, life force, will, vitality, purpose, life's direction, what and who we *really* are.

The Sun represents our basic urge for self-expression. It is the 'Solar energy cell' in a person's character, the Lord and giver of life, and symbolises the way in which an individual will shine out to the world. Our Sun is our personal identity and aspects to it from other components in the chart show the ease or otherwise of assuredness and confidence with which one will project and express one's individuality. The Sun sign will also show how an individual bounces back from setbacks and disappointments, their resilience and their general outward expression of energy.

The Sun is the archetype of the Father and represents the primary masculine principle in the natal chart. It indicates how we express and experience our masculine side, or animus, our conscious self, how we express ourselves creatively, our personal potential, individuality, self-expression and personal power. It has to do with courage, power, generosity, creativity, vitality, self-confidence, nobility, self-worth, dignity and strength of will. It symbolises authority and purpose, the *ruler*, and its potential is the peak of constructive maturity. It signifies self-sufficiency and abundance, containing enough energy to radiate warmth and give life to everything around it.

The sign in which one's Sun is posited, and its placement in the birth chart, strongly indicates the level and type of vitality available to the personality (the sign), and in which area of life this may be most strongly directed (the house).

The Sun in a natal chart is a powerful symbol because everything is filtered, at a conscious level, through it. It tells us what we need to do to feel fully alive, the type of engine 'driving' us, what we need to do to be authentic and to be fully functioning. Listening to the special message of one's Sun sign can provide one with greater direction, and a more dynamic energy and life purpose.

The symbol for the Sun ☉ depicts a circle with a dot or 'seed' at its centre, from which the core self, power, creativity and the first sparks of life can spring. The circle around this 'seed' represents spirit, symbolising wholeness, eternity and the never-ending flow of energy.

While the Moon, the night sky's luminary, represents the *soul*, the Sun, the day sky's luminary, represents our *spirit*.

There is a reason your Sun sign is otherwise known as your Star Sign - it's because, quite simply, the Sun *is* a star; in fact, it's the largest, brightest, shiniest one in Earth's known visible Universe. This book is about your Sun sign and how you can become much larger, glow with far more brilliance, and shine brighter than you ever dreamed possible. I wish you all the magic in the galaxy for your dreams to come true and your deepest wishes to become reality, through tapping into the amazing power and inherent potential of your Sun sign. So get set for a galactical ride through the lucky stars of your constellation - and may a shooting star cross the path in front of you as you go!

CANCER THE CRAB

★ Cardinal Water, Negative, Feminine, Feeling ★

"Loved ones are nurtured protectively"

Body & Health
Stomach, Breasts, Fluids, Membranes, Womb, Chest, Elbows

How Cancer Emanates its Life Force / Energy
Emotively, Intuitively, Protectively, with Feeling

Is Concerned With
★ Receptivity ★ Defence ★ Sensitivity ★ Home ★ ★ Protection ★ Comfort ★ Domesticity ★
★ Food ★ Nurturing ★ Mothering Instincts ★
★ Sentiments ★ Roots ★ Antiques ★
★ The Psychic Realm ★ Intuition ★ Feeling ★ Family ★ History, Nostalgia, Memory ★

Spiritual Cancer

Your Archetypal Universal Qualities
The Water Child, Mother, Nurturer

What You Refuse
To forget or to let go

What You Are an Authority On
Sustaining, Protecting and Preserving Capacities

The Main Senses Through Which You Experience Your Reality
Security, Home, Belonging, Memory, Intuition, Maternal

How You Love
Protectively, with Tenacity

Positive Characteristics
★ Shrewd ★ Intuitive ★ Dedicated ★
★ Excellent ★ Memory ★ Nourishing ★
★ Kind and Compassionate ★ Tenacious ★ Caring ★
Helpful ★ Sensitive to Need ★ Tender ★
★ Protective ★ Loyal ★ Imaginative ★
★ Values Home and Family Life ★

Negative Characteristics
★ Possessive and Clingy ★ Insular ★
★ Too Easily Hurt ★ Private ★ Insecure ★
★ Withdrawing ★ Crabby and Moody ★ Timid ★
★ Holds onto Past Insults and Hurts ★ ★ Overpowering
★ Manipulative ★ Over-protective ★ Smothering ★
★ Introspective ★ Hidden ★

To Bring Out Your Best
Cook a meal; build up a large savings account; spend quality time with your family; possess a home or space of your own; live by the sea; frolic in an ocean rock pool.

Spiritual Goals

To learn how to feel secure in oneself instead of seeking it externally outside of the self through clinginess and possessiveness; to share more of yourself and emerge from your shell; to allow others 'in'; to overcome shyness and over-sensitivity; to learn when and how to let go; to use your emotions constructively to help others.

CANCER

21 June - 22 July

Cardinal Water

Ruled by the Moon

"I FEEL"

Gemstones ◊ Moonstone, Pearl, Ruby

★ Emotional, security-seeking, moody, loving, persistent, intuitive, changeable, imaginative, receptive, maternal, loving, possessive, cautious, retentive, protective, loyal, private, sympathetic, unable to let go, sensitive, tenacious, dependent, reflective, home-loving, nurturing, insightful, touchy, snappy, crabby, hypersensitive, cowardly, shrewd, despondent, irritable, clingy, tender, psychic, kind, nostalgic ★

"The basic fact is that all sentient beings, particularly human beings, want happiness and do not want pain and suffering"
The Dalai Lama

CANCER

♋

**Changeable ★ Feeling ★ Moody
Protective ★ Tenacious ★ Private
Nostalgic ★ Imaginative**

Cancer is the sign of the Crab, a hard-shelled, soft-centred crustacean who skittles sideways and hides when feeling threatened or hurt. Protective, nurturing, emotional, clingy, intuitive, shrewd, changeable, motherly, moody and private are Cancers' most notable traits. Being a sensitive and feeling Water sign, this sign feels its way through life guided by its instincts and inner knowing, being either engulfed or empowered by its emotions in all situations. Tenacious and shrewd in both business and matters of the heart, Cancerians love to lead and to protect, two things which come naturally to them.

The Crab is home-loving, domestic and security-seeking, needing her family and home life to be running smoothly in order to function at her highest level. Moods are a strong feature of the imaginative Crab's spirit, and she needs plenty of love and understanding to keep her Watery nature in check. Cancer is sympathetic and clingy, often holding on with tight pincers which find it hard to let go, embracing and protecting her loved ones with a gentle but powerful force. The Crab lives in the past, being the most reminiscent, sentimental and nostalgic of all the signs, possessing an excellent memory but often remembering past hurts long after everyone else has moved on.

A nurturing lover, loyal friend and at times deeply private and hidden, Cancer is the fourth sign and the caring 'mother' of the zodiac, providing warmth, love, comfort and nourishment to anyone lucky enough to be the recipient.

KEY CONCEPTS
★ Hypersensitive to and absorbing of all feelings ★
★ Extremely fluctuating and changeable ★
★ Cares for others' needs and wants ★
★ Prone to hysteria, worry and irritability ★
★ Indulges in irrational and unfounded fears ★
★ Can be selfish and oblivious to all desires but own ★
★ Insular, veiled, inaccessible and private ★
★ Possessive, clingy and unable to release or let go ★
★ Psychic and impressionable ★
★ Avails of self to assist others ★
★ Holds the family together ★
★ Understands all human afflictions, weaknesses, shortcomings and conditions ★

SOME CORRESPONDENCES THAT ARE ASSOCIATED WITH CANCER

Breasts, the stomach, domestic life, family, cycles, bakers, motherhood, kitchens, food, creeks, plumbers, glassware, guesthouses, restaurants, tides, bakeries, digestive system, bathrooms, streams, housekeepers, mushrooms, vegetable growers, pearls, pearling, obstetrics, boats, sailors, hotels, mothers, storekeepers, boating, swimming, fertility, breeding, catering, collectors, fluids, cooks, grocers, real estate, nourishment, sentimentality, homes and homemakers, cooking, lakes, crabs and other shellfish, fruitfulness, and water. Take your pick and enjoy the ride!

QUOTES BY CANCERIANS

"Our deepest fear is not that we are inadequate. Our deepest fear is that we are powerful beyond measure. It is our light, not our darkness, that most frightens us. We ask ourselves, who am I to be brilliant, gorgeous, talented, fabulous? Actually, who are you *not* to be? Your playing small does not serve the world. There is nothing enlightened about shrinking so that other people won't feel insecure around you. … As we let our own Light shine, we unconsciously give others permission to do the same. As we are liberated from our own fear, our presence automatically liberates others" - Marianne Williamson (8 July 1952)

"My family really does come first. It always did and always will" - Meryl Streep (22 June 1949)

"The best and most beautiful things in the world cannot be seen or even touched - they must be felt with the heart" - Helen Keller (27 June 1880)

"Humans are by nature too complicated to be understood fully. So, we can choose either to approach our fellow human beings with suspicion or to approach them with an open mind, a dash of optimism and a great deal of candour" - Tom Hanks (9 July 1956)

"Approach love and cooking with reckless abandon" - Dalai Lama (6 July 1935)

"Each generation imagines itself to be more intelligent than the one that went before it, and wiser than the one that comes after it" - George Orwell (25 June 1903)

"I like to listen. I have learned a great deal from listening carefully. Most people never listen" - Ernest Hemmingway (21 July 1899)

"Security is mostly a superstition. It does not exist in nature … Avoiding danger is no safer in the long run than outright exposure. Life is either a daring adventure, or nothing" - Helen Keller

"I'm a Cancer; I'm music-passionate. I like long walks on the beach" - Will Ferrell (16 July 1967)

"It's great to be a blonde. With low expectations, it's very easy to surprise people" - Pamela Anderson (1 July 1967)

"The biggest disease this day and age is that of people feeling unloved" - Princess Diana (1 July 1961)

"There is nothing to writing. All you do is sit down at a typewriter and bleed" - Ernest Hemmingway

"Let us be grateful to people who make us happy. They are the charming gardeners who make our souls blossom" - Marcel Proust (10 July 1871)

"My religion is very simple. My religion is kindness" - Dalai Lama

"I used to think that the worst thing in life was to end up alone. It's not. The worst thing in life is to end up with people who make you feel alone" - Robin Williams (21 July 1951)

"Aren't we all striving to be overpaid for what we do?" - Will Ferrell

"Eventually you just have to realise that you're living for an audience of one. I'm not here for anyone else's approval" - Pamela Anderson

"You're only given a little spark of madness. You mustn't lose it" - Robin Williams

"I disagree with people who think you learn more from getting beat up than you do from winning" - Tom Cruise (3 July 1962)

"There is no friend as loyal as a book" - Ernest Hemmingway

"If your actions inspire others to dream more, learn more, do more, or become more, you are a leader" - John Quincy Adams (11 July 1767)

"The only thing worse than being blind is having sight but no vision" - Helen Keller

"The mass of men live lives of quiet desperation" - Henry David Thoreau (12 July 1817)

"I love what I do. I take great pride in what I do. And I can't do something halfway, three-quarters, nine-tenths. If I'm going to something, I go all the way" - Tom Cruise

"Comedy can be a cathartic way to deal with personal trauma" - Robin Williams

"Being a princess is not all it's cracked up to be" - Princess Diana

"God, grant me the serenity to accept the things I cannot change, the courage to change the things I can, and the wisdom to know the difference" - *Serenity Prayer*, Reinhold Neibuhr (21 June 1892)

"If you have built castles in the air, your work need not be lost. That is where they should be. Now put the foundations under them" - Henry David Thoreau

"Happiness is as a butterfly, which when pursued, is always beyond our grasp, but which if you will sit down quietly, may alight upon you" - Nathaniel Hawthorne (4 July 1804)

"Go confidently in the direction of your dreams. Live the life you have imagined" - Henry David Thoreau

"I don't go by the rule book. I rule from the heart, not the head" - Princess Diana

"The only thing standing between you and your goal is the bullsh*t story you keep telling yourself as to why you can't achieve it" - Jordan Belfort (9 July 1962)

"I love to be alone. I never found a companion that was so companionable as solitude" - Henry David Thoreau

"One cannot consent to creep when one feels an impulse to soar" - Helen Keller

THE CANCER CONSTELLATION

The signs of the zodiac are the twelve symbolic features that ancient people imagined while observing the heavens. They saw shapes, patterns, faces, and natural and supernatural beings in the stars, from which they established, over centuries, a kind of celestial hierarchy and system based upon their observations. Groupings of stars became constellations, and twelve of these constellations make up the zodiac, a Greek word meaning 'circle of animals', that we know today.

Star constellations are not really self-contained groups but are particularly bright stars that give the appearance of being close together and form distinctive patterns. These are the patterns that over the ages have been identified as animals, deities or mythological figures and heroes. The stars are the living past. We receive their light long after it has left the star itself and so they are a good focus for escaping from the parameters of time. Their stellar influence is analogous with the aura, the bio/psychic energy field surrounding humans, animals, plants, crystals and even places. These individual energy systems interact with the energy waves emanated by other people, and even the cosmic rays emitted by planetary bodies, for psychic energies are not limited by time or distance.

The cluster of stars we know as Cancer the Crab is a small, faint constellation, but both its shape and its glyph contain a representation of the crab's claws. It contains Sirius, one of the brightest stars in the zodiac, in its constellation. It also contains a cluster of stars known as the 'Praesaepe', the manger or crib. Aside from Praesaepe, the Crab is composed of only five or six stars. It is best seen during the evenings of early (northern hemisphere) spring when it is almost directly overhead.

WISHING UPON YOUR STAR

The practice of wishing upon a star is familiar to most of us, and is a mystical superstition that is ingrained in many of us from childhood. As a night-time ritual, you can wish upon your own sign's constellation or that of the sign whose energies you wish to call forth; indeed, you can wish upon any constellation you feel an affinity with. If you can't see a particular constellation in your night sky, you can always meditate on it in your mind, or you can use the traditional technique of wishing upon the first star you see, while reciting the popular rhyme: *Star light, star bright, first star I see tonight, I wish I may, I wish I might, have the wish I make this night!* Any one of the three rituals will hold power for your own special wish. Good luck!

THE CANCERIAN SYMBOL ♋

Astrology uses symbols or 'glyphs' to represent the planets and signs. The glyph is made up of shapes representing the energy and physical matter of which the Universe is composed, and how these shapes are used in each symbol provide hints as to the properties of the sign or planet it represents.

The ancient view was that there were five elements: Fire, Water, Air, Earth and Ether (or Spirit). Ether is invisible energy, while the four tangible elements are known as 'matter'. Ether, as pure energy, cannot be influenced by any of the physical/matter elements, although it surrounds them and indeed fuels them. The Greek philosopher and scientist Aristotle regarded this idea as a circle (Ether/Spirit) with a cross (matter) in the centre. This glyph is used in astrology as a symbol for Earth, and the cycle of life. All the symbols used in astrology represent the relationship between energy and the 'matter' elements.

The glyph for Cancer, which consists of two circles and two curved lines, is a typical Ether glyph. The half-circle, or crescent, depicts the soul force or consciousness. This is a combination of the Solar circle and the Lunar crescent. All curved lines, whether half or complete circles, are considered emotional and responsive. These two inverted and intertwined loops resemble the breasts, the spiral of shells, or the Crab's claws. This glyph also brings to mind the symbol of the Chinese yin and yang.

Cancer's glyph shows the same duality as its preceding sign, Gemini, in its passive form, shown by the horizontal lines, but imbued with a new potentiality, shown by the small added circles, giving the idea of two seeds, from the combination of which a mature organism can grow. The symbol of the Crab, whose hard shell protects its soft interior and whose tenacious grip is like the hold of the emotional life upon humans, aptly sums up the characteristics of your sign. Cancer rules the stomach and a crab is practically a walking stomach. Those subject to shifting moods are often called 'crabby'. The baby's protective cradle is sometimes called a 'crib'.

THE AGE OF CANCER ★ 8000 - 2000 BC

The Age of Cancer was a period of time during which people began to build dwellings and the emphasis of home and family life followed naturally. The Age of Cancer was believed to have coincided with the great floods described in the literature of nearly every significant culture, including in the Bible. Many cultures at this time had religious practices that involved the worship of the Moon, ruler of Cancer, and honoured its cycles. People began to observe the phases of the Moon and its effects on the tides. In some cultures, the Lunar cycles were linked with spiritual phenomena and were also used to measure time. In China, this still plays a role in today's world: in the modern Chinese calendar, the Chinese New Year occurs at the second new Moon after the Winter Solstice.

During the Age of Cancer, people formed more complex societies and became less nomadic. It is also a time associated with early matriarchal societies, as well as the start of agriculture that involved the cultivation of crops and the keeping of domesticated animals. People also recognised a growing need for protection against the elements, wild animals and human enemies and invaders. Fertility cults and rites were widespread, characterised by carvings of rotund women with large breasts, showing a strong influence of Cancer, which is ruled by the Moon and signifies fertility, the realm of the home and of course the breasts. During this time, people learned to spin, weave and make pottery, a trend that began in China, Egypt, Mesopotamia and India.

THE RUNDOWN & LESSONS
SOME QUIRKS, ODDITIES, UNIQUE CHARACTERISTICS AND IDIOSYNCRASIES OF CANCER

> "Children born under the sign (of Cancer) are extremely sensitive, and will only thrive if given plenty of fresh air and sunshine. The sea calls them …"
>
> ***Linda Goodman's Sun Signs*, Linda Goodman, Pan Books, 1968**

There are two types of thinkers: what I like to call 'right-brainers' and 'left-brainers'. The left hemisphere of the human brain deals with things such as control of speech, verbal functions, reason, logic, mathematics, linear concepts, details, sequences, the intellect and analysis; the right hemisphere is concerned with spatial, music, holistic, artistic concepts, as well as simultaneity and intuition. You could go on to say that the left brain is masculine or yang in quality, and the right brain is feminine or yin in quality. Based upon these very simplistic outlines, it can be further stated that Water sign Cancer dwells mainly in the right hemisphere, with a bit of left thrown in for good measure. Indeed, your shrewd intelligence should never be underestimated.

The feeling nature of Water highlights emotion rather than logic. Cancer is largely motivated by feelings. Negative, cool, moist and phlegmatic, an enterprising (Cardinal) nurturing (Water) approach characterises the sign of the Crab.

There is something exquisitely feminine about the Cancerian nature. As soft and enveloping as the summer rain into which they are born (in the Northern Hemiterpene at least), they contain, protect and love whatever and whoever is close to them with the firm grip of a Crab's claw. But these are not always soft characters, for although they hide a tender inner self with their hard outer shell, they are fearless defenders for those they hold dear. But because you are rarely upfront or showy, you can be easily overlooked. What lies beneath your shell may be well hidden and difficult to fathom, but you don't always scuttle under the nearest rock or into the tightest crevice to escape the many dangers of Earthly life; no, you will often be found clinging, fighting, and bearing your claws, challenging others to come closer - if they dare! A Cancerian would never hurt anyone unnecessarily, but you will give a sharp nip if you feel you've been slighted. Not only that, but you will keep a grip on the accused for a long time afterwards; your memory is impeccable and you dwell for the most part in the past. Perhaps the animal symbol for your sign should've been an elephant, for Cancerians *never* forget.

Cancer is the first of the Watery signs, and is ruled by the Moon. There is little doubt that Cancerians are not the easiest of characters to understand or to bear with. At your best you are kind, helpful, affable, thoughtful and understanding, but you can also be - for no apparent reason - bad-tempered, snappy, moody and short with anyone who speaks to you, and sometimes refuse to speak at all. Not by accident have expressions like 'crabbed', 'crabby' and 'old crab' scuttled into our vocabulary. In one version of the Oxford Dictionary, a definition of 'crabbed' is offered as: 'perversely intricate; hard to make sense of; difficult to decipher'. Indeed, the Cancerian soul can be hard to figure out. She may not always know where she's going, but she knows when she's got to go. And so she scurries about, sometimes frontward, other times backward, then sideways, nibbling at bits and pieces of the life experiences she finds in her path, because she instinctively knows she needs to absorb any lessons and nourishment deemed sufficient to strengthen her shell.

Like the changing faces of your ruler, the Moon, sometimes you are willing to listen with great sympathy to other people's problems and offer what you can to help, while at others you will find it extremely difficult to listen to anyone else's tales of woe but your own. This is the Cancerian's eternal conflict: positive, kind, protective on the one hand - harsh, sullen, ill-tempered on the other. You tend to swing like a pendulum between the two extremes, and like the crab, will scuttle sideways to evade a confronting situation, making you difficult to catch - and to understand, for you never approach things directly or headlong. You also align yourself to the Moon's cycles whether you realise it or not, and can swing between being outwardly compassionate and self-pitying. You should never be mistaken for a wallflower though, as you are tough as nails and incredibly ambitious if you are passionate about something or someone. A part of you longs for success and achievement, but a bigger part of you will be pulled towards the home. Indeed, home is of vital importance to Cancer. Any disruption in this realm can cause anxiety, worry and emotional angst that affects every other part of your life. Moving home can be traumatic for you, as you strive above all for security and comfort, and you are sentimental about that place you call 'home'.

Cancer's basis for understanding her world is almost always emotional. Cancer feels; she rarely thinks - rationally, at least. When spiritually evolved, Cancerians make excellent psychic workers and healers, such is your need to sustain and help others.

Despite the rather solemn and emotional picture I have thus far drawn up of the Cancerian character, in actuality you possess one of the zaniest senses of humour of the whole zodiac. In fact, your fears and worries are almost always well-covered by your nutty Lunar humour, and no one tells a joke better than you; this Lunar humour runs deep. Your funny side is all the more surprising when it bursts out so unexpectedly from your normally quiet, make-no-waves, gentle self. That is why your unassuming manner should not fool anyone, for you can be as batty and dry as a well-timed comedian, you just both hide it and time it with great skill.

Because you are seldom direct, you can become overwhelmed by emotions to the point that you may become irrational, repressed or impaired in some way. This is the cause of most of your suffering. But you do tend to suffer in silence, partly to protect yourself (or so you think) and partly to protect and nurture your loved ones. Any anguish will be deeply disguised and life will go on as normal as you like to appear strong and sure in all situations, especially those involving family dynamics.

Moon-ruled Crabs are nurturers, always willing to offer an understanding ear. If you don't immediately scurry away at the first sign of danger, when it comes to defending yourself you would prefer a quick nip in the form of a well-placed word (after which you may duck back into your shell and feign indifference); Cancerians are usually intelligent, articulate and word-wise.

Being a Cardinal sign, you are the most dynamic of the Water signs, acting on a combination of feelings and shrewdness to secure yourself a safe, cosy niche. Once in this haven, you lavish those close to you - as well as all your special possessions and collectibles - with abundant and tender love.

Cancerians are renowned for being psychic, for you are particularly open to the influx of vast Universal forces, which channel themselves into the confines of the Cancerian's individual consciousness whether or not you choose to be such a channel.

Cancer is also often associated with maternal instincts and motherhood. In Cancer, the concept of the relationship between the mother and the child is honoured and celebrated, and is a relationship which is established once the egg is fertilised. Researchers claim that this relationship between the foetus and the mother during the nine-month prenatal period has dramatic and long-lasting effects from birth to adulthood. This is essentially where the mother creates the relationship with her child and the child is receptive to all input - physically, emotionally and psychically. This is also where the umbilical cord is established and it does not necessarily get cut following birth, at least not on a psychic level. Indeed, for some people the psychic umbilical cord remains linked to the mother throughout life, and for those living the Cancerian experience, this is often the case. This profound attachment can be attributed to the mother's not letting go of the child, the child's inability to detach from the mother, or both. In the sign of Cancer, we are surrounded by Water (as is the foetus in the womb), feeling, vibrations and sensitivity - and strong absorption will naturally occur in this environment.

Cancer shares her need for security with the sign of Taurus, another security-oriented sign. however, Taurus needs it in the physical, material realm, while Cancer seeks it in the emotional realm. As well as security, Cancer yearns for nourishment. In medical astrology, your sign rules the breasts and the womb - the two biological organs that exist primarily to provide a safe 'home' and nourishment to the developing infant. And so nourishment, to Cancer, is important thereafter, and throughout life. However, you are vulnerable to over-eating and other such excess-indulgences, using substances in a way that is damaging to yourself, often to compensate for a lack of emotional sustenance in your life.

Cancerians are romantic, home- and family-oriented and tenacious, but they are easily shaken and possess an often impenetrable timidity based around fear. You are arguably the most sensitive of all the zodiac signs, and your feelings can even be wounded by a harsh look or a rough tone of voice. You are moved to tears and withdrawal by even the slightest hurt, but your resilience always has you coming back out of your shell once the wave has washed over. But you will never forget it, for you hold each emotion tightly with your retentive memory and renowned ability to *absorb*. You also have a liking - and a pressing need - for privacy, solitude and retreat, and like a real Crab, you seek out any of these states if you are feeling uncertain, vulnerable, sad or despairing.

As well as your urge for time alone on a regular basis, you are a well of secrecy. Your compassion and empathy are deep, knowing, highly intuitive and absorbent. However, in your relationships and exchanges, these qualities travel a one-way street. You guard your inner feelings fiercely and protectively, and although you will gather all the information you can on the emotions and nuances of close others, soaking them up like a sponge, others may find it hard to penetrate your own feelings, rarely being able to decipher your private workings. While you gather much knowledge on others, you seldom judge, as you are most concerned with gathering, absorbing, sorting and reflecting.

Tenacious and shrewd in both business and matters of the heart, Cancerians love to lead and to protect, two things which come naturally to them. You often give an appearance of timidity, laziness, receptivity and passivity, but appearances can be deceiving and you are stronger than others - and indeed you yourself - realise. You are far from inactive, you are just not overt about anything that you do. You may seem to be swanning or lolling around, but you should never be underestimated, for the element of Water is invariably most active and powerful *under* the surface, in those deep undercurrents that we can't always see.

As much as you love your whole home, there is always a special part of it that you like to keep to yourself, a corner or room to which you can retreat, for example. Although you love to share and give of yourself, you tend to have reclusive tendencies, and the secure place that you choose will be a space in which you can reminisce, daydream, wallow, recall memories, or create. In this sacred space, you should always be left alone and undisturbed, for if someone disrupts this special time and place in any way, your deeply coveted need for privacy will send you back into your hidden world for an even longer period.

This withdrawal can happen quite often as you've strong emotional reactions. These strong emotions can be directed positively into caring for and protecting others, particularly your family and loved ones. When you're feeling an emotional equilibrium you enjoy giving to others, sharing warm and loving moments, and also enjoy your own company. In particular, though you yearn to look after those you love, nursing them through illness, cooking a favourite meal or curling up on a lounge with them. You've strong home-making urges, and your home will be a great source of comfort to your friends and family. Indeed, you are very attached to the home and family and will have many experiences and changes in connection with your place of domestic residence.

Moods are a big thing for the imaginative Crab's spirit, and you need plenty of love and understanding to keep your Watery nature in check. The Crab is the most attachment-seeking and clingy of all the zodiac signs, and due to its Cardinal nature will not be shy in finding others to merge with. But it must be acknowledged that the ongoing process of absorbing the feelings of others and the human environment necessitates the purging of those feelings as well. However, Cancer finds it difficult to be objective, much less detach from anything, as attested by its claws. The Crab's delicate character is almost always weighed down by circumstances or relationships of the past that she simply refuses to let go of. You may suffer from issues arising from co-dependence and 'smother love', but because your intentions are always good and your heart so giving, positive karma will always be on your side. If you refuse to learn the lessons contained in your suffering however, misunderstandings and resentments will inevitably surface and prove toxic to your life. When your self is threatened, you tend to withdraw into a womb-like environment where your emotions can be processed and understood. Even when you do finally re-emerge, you will remain secretive and vulnerable, for these are embedded facets of your character that are difficult, if not impossible, to purge and release.

Cancer deals with any kind of attachment, love, dependency and family - in all their forms. There is a complexity and paradox in your sign however; Cardinality is outgoing and purposeful, where Water is emotional and receptive. The sign itself is symbolised by the crab and we can learn much about Cancer's nature from this creature. Living in the corners of rocky pools and in the sand, it is timid, insecure, hides swiftly, and yet has pincer claws which can be used aggressively. The crab has a tough outer shell but is soft and vulnerable underneath; similarly, many Cancerians tend to protect their emotions under this hard shell. There is a strong mothering instinct within this sign which can express with deeply caring emotions and sensitivity, but it can also smother and envelope. Crabs move sideways, and this symbolises the indirectness which the Cancerian often uses as a way of reconciling its active-passive paradox.

Although you are fond of change, variable in mood and impressionable, you are capable of extraordinary tenacity. Imaginative, sociable, loving of ease, peace and home life, you are often dismissed as being sulky, shy and weepy, but you are in fact a force to be reckoned with. Underneath your protective shell is a kind and caring nature, and yet at the very heart of Cancer there is a rock-hard centre of determination and a generous measure of self-interest. And this determination, fuelled by your forceful Cardinality, means you'll forge ahead, albeit in a subtle way, rather than taking a backseat in life. Water, being hard to contain, will always find a way of going exactly where it wants or needs to go. Cancer's 'self-interest' also means the interests of close loved ones. You are driven by the need to nurture and protect those dear to you, and will defend them as fiercely as you would defend yourself. In essence, you're a gentle bully if there is such a thing, who's chivvying and worrying and smothering and snapping always comes out of loving concern. You have a maternal protectiveness capable of fierce action, tenaciously protecting the lives of kith and kin: not only children, but your family as a whole, the tribe and the immediate community.

Cancer is a Cardinal sign and Cardinality implies drive, initiative and impetus. Water is a powerful force and, when allied with impetus, it can become the most dangerous medium there can be. For Water puts out Fire, combines with Air in hurricanes, sweeps away Earth in landslides, joins forces with the Earth to create tsunamis, and an excess of Water will burst river banks and dams. The power that Cancer wields should therefore never be underestimated. Her shyness is not timidity, but rather a cloak for her feelings; a protective armour build to insulate against emotional exposure; and any tendency towards lachrymosity is prompted by your soft heart and excessive sensitivity, for you are the most empathetic sign of the zodiac. Ruled by the Lunar sphere, your frequent changes of mood and whims are caused by the Moon's rapid passage each month through all twelve signs of the zodiac, and hence through the archetypal emotional human experiences represented by each. Indeed, this cycle colours your responses, emotions and instincts in twelve different ways.

Highly imaginative, Cancer is often creative and artistic, and gifted with a shrewd knack of making money and the even better facility of hanging onto it. But money isn't the only thing you hang onto. You find it difficult to relinquish anything, and carry around with you your whole life, its memories, old friends, long-ago hurts and wounds, and past lovers, even old books that are so well-read they're dog-eared and torn - but also dusty. You take comfort from your possessions, especially the childhood ones which evoke feelings of nostalgia, and seek solace in the security of your surroundings. In fact, Cancer is deeply affected by early emotional experiences.

It is an extremely rare Cancer who will relinquish a treasured object or memory, and you cling with determination and loyalty, refusing to let go of anything, even if it no longer serves you. It is also a rare Cancer who will walk out on a relationship, marriage or family; as you are never direct, you would prefer to use mind games to 'manipulate' the other into leaving *you* instead, so you are not burdened with the heavier end of the guilt. Your strategy is always to move in every other direction than straight ahead, and although you are very in touch with your feelings, it can be difficult for you to express them in a straightforward manner. You play the shifting game, shuffling from side to side, until your prey is right where you want it, and then you will cleverly and quickly lunge forward, take hold with your pincers and refuse to release your prize until you have made every last ounce of use out of it - which sometimes never happens, as you never truly run out of uses for a loved one.

At times you are rather shy and reserved, but in every Cancerian there is a desire for publicity and recognition, which you may well attain given your incredibly shrewd and tenacious nature. Once having made your mind along a certain course of action, you are able to hang on where others let go.

Generous and giving, you are easily touched by someone in need. However, you are not impulsive, and out of self-preservation and perhaps your sheer

Watery wisdom, you will only distribute your time, efforts, energy, money or emotions after you have weighed it all up in your soft centre first. When it comes to benevolent acts of giving, you are discerning if nothing else.

As a feeling Water sign, you are apt to be *too* receptive to the influence of those around you, subconsciously taking on their woes and conditions, which accounts for many of the moods you find yourself in that even you don't understand. And whilst persistent, you are easily discouraged, and tend to brood over mistakes instead of learning from them and picking yourself up to try again; once you have fallen, it will take a while until you are ready to take the chance again. You are also inclined to be a great worrier, and your imaginative powers are considerable - and while this may aggravate your tendency to worry, it can act as a great release.

Although you possess a strong leaning towards security and comfort, you are also decidedly fond of change, variable in mood and easily influenced, yet curiously, capable of extraordinary tenacity. Gently sociable, you have a loving of ease, affection and harmony.

Overall, you are adaptable, cautious, economical and determined, and your intuition is very marked, with decided psychic and even occult leanings. Beneath your hard outer shell is a soft, delicate, vulnerable and deeply caring spirit - if you can come out of hiding long enough for it to truly shine.

LESSONS TO BE LEARNED FOR GREATER POWER, ENLIGHTENMENT & LUCK

Cancerian problems and ultimate undoings arise through your emotional over-sensitivity, your inability to let go of the past or past hurts, your possessiveness, the 'cotton-woolling' of your children or those you love, letting your vulnerabilities consume you, and your tendency to hold onto security at all costs. While you are protective of loved ones and family, you are also inclined to smothering and jealousy, which are born out of inner insecurities. You also tend to be private and hidden, sharing little of yourself, and become particularly so when hurt or feeling threatened, imagined or otherwise. Opening up a little and quite literally coming out of your shell by embracing greater courage will go a long way to manifesting the love and emotional fulfilment you so desire from others. Holding onto the past can also present problems for you, and although challenging for the past-dwelling Crab, it is important for you to learn perspective and live more in the present. Co-dependence can become a burden without you even realising it has crept up upon you, because by then it is often too late and too entrenched to address it effectively. Finding a way to nurture yourself rather than relying upon others for emotional buoyancy, is the first step to walking your more soulful path in life.

Your greatest strength and your greatest weakness can also be found in your extreme sensitivity, coupled with your urge to create and preserve life. From these flow your love of home, domesticity and children, your instinct for protection, and your urge for permanence. That Cancer sense of 'I Feel' gives you a psychic antenna which picks up impulses and atmospheres, both from within yourself and from others. But unless this sensitivity is guided by faith in the wider life-force and directed by faith in your-self, it can lead you into dangerous waters. Confusion, fear, sensationalism, worry and slavery to every emotional whim can characterise the negative Cancerian. Being ruled by the changeable and fluctuating Lunar influence, your feelings wax and wane and your childhood experiences and memories run deep. Your sensitivity and deeply feeling nature, positively expressed, casts light and inspiration wherever you go, but you must heal old wounds and control your moods to be at your best.

THE THREE DECANS OF CANCER

Decans are thirty-six groups of stars that rise in a particular order on the horizon throughout each Earth rotation. These decans were developed in Egypt thousands of years ago. The rising of each decan marked the beginning of a new 'decanal hour' of the night for these ancient people, and eventually three decans were assigned to each zodiac sign. Each decan covers ten degrees of the zodiac wheel, and is ruled by different planetary rulers that rule over the other two signs of the same element (and a traditional ruler, when only seven of the planetary bodies were known). Decans continued to be used throughout the Ages, in astrology and in magic, but many modern astrologers, for whatever reasons, tend to disregard them. Following are brief descriptions for each decan of Cancer. Which one do you belong to? Can you relate to the description and the energies of your decan's ruling planet?

FIRST DECAN CANCER ★ June 21 - July 1

Ruler ★ Venus (traditional *) / Moon (modern)

Keyword ★ Emotional

First Decan Cancers' Three Special Tarot Cards
The Chariot, Queen of Cups & Two of Cups

Birthdays in this decan range from 21st June to 1st July. This is the Cancer decan, ruled by Venus * and the Moon. Cancerians born during this decan possess a bright, sociable, imaginative and receptive character. The alliance of Venus, ruler of this decan, and the Moon, ruling planet of Cancer, intensifies the emotional and sensual qualities relating to your sign. This influence can make you hypersensitive, over-reliant on others for emotional support, dreamy, pleasant, tender, charming, anxious and prone to worry. You may also be inclined to dramatize and idealise the past and your feelings. Generous, imaginative and creative, you have a great sense of intuition and derive self-satisfaction through helping others. You seek security for yourself and your loved ones, but you may be clingy and sensitive, which clouds your objectivity and gives rise to a heightened vulnerability where you are too easily hurt.

SECOND DECAN CANCER ★ July 2 - 12

Ruler ★ Mercury (traditional *) / Mars (modern)

Keyword ★ Sympathetic

Second Decan Cancers' Three Special Tarot Cards The Chariot, Queen of Cups & Three of Cups

Birthdays in this decan range from 2nd July to 12th July. This is the Scorpio decan, sub-ruled by Mars. The Mars influence signifies force, vigour, energy, power and vitality. Therefore, the stronger characteristics of Cancer are exhibited in your personality. Although possessive, insecure and emotional, you are deeply caring, generous and protective. Because you are inclined to demonstrate the stronger of the naturally reticent and soft Cancerian nature, you also tend to be moody, alternating between being down and being optimistic. You are also prone to going off on flights of fancy and being too nostalgic and clingy, clinging to the past, a person or an ideal, and you need to be more practical. The Mercurial influence ensures that your intelligence will be refined, and you will tend towards either genius or laziness. You are also resourceful and inquisitive, and possess a strong imagination, an enlightened conscience and a deep capacity for empathy.

THIRD DECAN CANCER ★ July 13 - 22

Ruler ★ Moon (traditional *) / Jupiter (modern)

Keyword ★ Sensitive

Third Decan Cancers' Three Special Tarot Cards
The Chariot, King of Wands & Four of Cups

Birthdays in this decan range from 13th July to 22nd July. This is the Pisces decan, ruled by the Moon * and Jupiter. Cancerians born during this decan are characterised by a love of knowledge and spirituality. In fact, Jupiter's influence will gift you with a great deal of intelligence and gain through education and travel; you would do well to make the most of this endowment. However, you may also be prone to melancholia, moodiness and negativity at times, being unable to see the brighter side of life through clouded emotions. This is when Jupiter's influence as a Great Benefic can assist - by drawing out your inner optimism and hope.

The decan's traditional ruler based on the Chaldean order of the planets

YOUR ELEMENT ★ WATER

According to the *Oxford English Dictionary*, the word *element* has a mysterious origin, and was first found in Greek texts meaning 'complex whole' or 'a single unit made up of many parts'. From the ancient up to medieval times, there were only four elements - Earth, Air, Fire and Water - and the occult-oriented also believed in a fifth: Spirit, or Ether. (Cornelius Agrippa called Spirit the 'quintessence'.)

Alchemy is a tradition of visions and dreams, and images can combine on different levels of reality. Alchemists have long used images in their illustrations to express the enigma and mystery of their art, and to include all dimensions of our experience. The traditional worlds of Earth, Water, Fire and Air symbolise these dimensions very well. Broadly speaking, and in human terms, Earth corresponds to the level of the body and the senses, Water to the flow of thoughts and feelings, Fire to inspiration and energy, and Air to the world of the higher mind and intellect. Each of these worlds has its own realm of imagery. Cancer belongs to the realm of the Water element.

★ The Emotional Group ★

The Path to SPIRITUALITY

Focused on Emotion and Feelings

Alchemical Associations ★ The Subconscious, Quicksilver and the Colour White

Key Attributes ★ Sensitivity, Flexibility, Intuition, Creativity, Feeling

Symbolism ★ Healing, Reflection and Cleansing

Governed by ★ The Soul and the Feelings

Water Characteristics ★ Subjective, Emotional, Intuitive, Sensitive, Imaginative, Receptive

★ THE MAGIC OF WATER ★

Water is the flow of emotions, the tide that carries you out to sea and will bring you back to a safe shore after your whimsical adventures. It can be placid or tempestuous, and without it life cannot flourish. It can cause your dreams to carry you away on the waves, without anchoring your aspirations. You can sink or swim in Water, having nothing to cling to for support, as it has no form, shaping itself into its surroundings. It needs a container to prevent your dreams being swept away; cups, goblets and bowls are often associated with water, and the term 'Holy Grail' describes your greatest desires.

The sage is like water.
Water is good, nourishes all things,
and does not compete with them.
It dwells in humble places that others disdain;
hence it is close to the Tao.
In his dwelling, the sage loves the earth.
In his mind, he loves what is profound.
In his associations, he is kind and gentle.

In his speech, he is sincere.
In his ruling, he is just.
In business, he is proficient.
In his action, he is timely.
Because he does not compete,
he does not find fault in others.
Lao Tzu (604-517 BC)
Tao Te Ching, **VIII**

★ KEYWORDS ★

Impressionable, compassionate, reflective, insightful, merging, fertile, receptive, absorbing, responsive, habitual, perceptive, secretive, submissive, possessive, nurturing, sensitive, clingy, dependent, instinctive, emotional, sympathetic, intriguing, protective, empathetic, psychic, mysterious *

* All these words don't necessarily describe all three Water signs. Pisces, for example, is not possessive, and Scorpio is not submissive.

Water is the most important element of all, for without it there would be no life on planet Earth. Without Water the land would not be fruitful or fertile, but dry and sterile. It has long been revered as the wellspring of life, enabling human civilisations to grow and flourish across the planet. The ancients understood the generative energy inherent in Water, and it has given rise to many myths, stories, superstitions and symbolism. For example, the chalice, a vessel for holding this element, is a legendary symbol of abundance and spiritual power. The Moon and its compelling influence on the seas and female reproductive cycles, is strongly linked with the Water element and its deeply feminine nature.

As the ultimate source of life and growth, Water is the most significant element in terms of regeneration and metamorphosis. Water follows a relatively unchanging cycle, going from a liquid state to a solid state, and according to scientific observations, reproduces itself around thirty-four times in the course of the terrestrial year. Under the combined influence of the movement of the Earth's rotation upon itself and of gravity, water shapes the Earth's surface. The perpetual motions and meandering courses of all the bodies of water on the surface of the globe, as well as the numerous currents, are caused by this terrestrial rotation, and also by the movements of the Moon around our planet. By the same token that water is the source of life - by drinking it or immersing yourself in it, you can regain your strength, satisfy a primary need, quench your thirst, be regenerated, and be washed and cleansed.

Water is the Universal Solvent, and the Universal Coagulant in the alchemical laboratory of nature. The Sun of Life, the Ego, passes through the waters of parturition in three definite stages symbolised by the Watery signs. They are the most primitive of all the animals depicted in the zodiac: the scorpion, the fish and the crab. The different astrological animal and human symbols, are said to represent the hierarchical instincts (e.g. aquatic, deep, dark) and the temperament of each creature or human type - our primal, instinctive and unconscious sides. Two of the Water signs - Scorpio and Cancer - are symbolised by half land-half water creatures, amphibious and flexible, but the Fish that represents the sign of Pisces can't breathe air and must live eternally in the cool water, sometimes muddy, sometimes clear, but always flowing.

In Greek mythology, Poseidon (Neptune to the Romans) rules the oceanic and water domains. Symbols and images most associated with the Water element include mermaids, wells, reservoirs, swimming, fish, crabs, lakes, rivers, dolphins, whales, diving, water-skiing and boating.

Water has long been associated with the powers of birth and regeneration, representing the feelings and healing energy. Ancient people built their settlements close to the life-giving rivers, streams and springs that became the source of several magical traditions and beliefs. In most cultures, wells, lakes and ponds were worshipped and venerated. Offerings were dropped into the watery depths in return for blessings - a ritual that survives today in the form of a wishing well.

Pulled by the Moon, the tides of Water can help you attune to change. The unpredictable nature of the waves and tides can be overwhelming however, and it's for this reason that Water brings powerful emotions to the surface, where they can be purged. Working with Water in your daily magic rituals can restore your spirit, increase your sensitivity, awareness and receptivity, and gently renew your faith in the flow of the Universe.

Astrologically, Water is associated with the feeling principle and function, representing the emotional realm. Its primary motivating force is deep yearnings. It is characterised by emotional depths, compassion and perceptions. Water signs are sensitive, experiencing life through their feelings. Attuned to delicate nuances, they can be dependent and vulnerable, often misinterpreting signals through the bias of their own feelings. When the intuitive function is working well, Watery signs can access an inner level of knowing that goes beyond the five physical senses.

Water is a paradoxical element and represents integration, dependence, merging, blending and union. Cancer represents personal development, Scorpio represents interpersonal development, and Pisces represents transpersonal development. The Water signs, living in the fluid world of emotion and feeling, express themselves in these differing ways: Cancer, through a great nurturing compassion, especially in home and family affairs; Scorpio, through its enormous sexual intensity and capacity, and its fascination for, and immersion in, the ultimate forces of life and death; and Pisces, through its acute sensitivity to the environment and its strongly developed depth of subconscious Universal undercurrents. The Water signs are feminine in polarity, introverted in expression.

Water signs are empathetic, attuned to others' feelings, and reflect the world around them as a reaction to how they feel. They experience the world subjectively. Water knows no boundaries and locates itself in the past, giving it a strong sense of memory and past experience. Often vulnerable to and overwhelmed by their emotions, their most appropriate outlets are expressed spiritually and artistically, or alternatively, to withdraw, hide, protect, deny, escape or defend.

Water, symbolic of the 'Great Mother', is the fountain of life and the source of all things, associated with birth, transformation, purification and movement. Deep, purifying and cleansing, it can symbolise the unending cascade of spiritual energy. But this movement can have its downside: although on the surface Water signs may appear calm, docile and placid, underneath there can be restlessness and deeper motivations brewing, for like the ocean, Watery people have many cross-currents. They are fearful of any form of confinement, and can therefore be extremely secretive about their true intentions or emotional undercurrents, making them at once enigmatic and mysterious.

As the element suggests, Water is sometimes turbulent, sometimes flowing, sometimes deep and murky, merges with its surroundings, and almost always fluid. Psychic, penetrative and intuitive, Water signs rely on instincts rather than logic. Acutely aware of the pain, feelings, suffering and thoughts of others, they are extremely sympathetic and will often put others' needs ahead of their own. Indeed, Water signs have an immense insight into human nature, making it hard for others to 'hide' around them; they dig, probe and 'feel' around to get to secrets and hidden matters. Although inherently private, Water signs can always be counted on for emotional support, sound advice and a receptive ear. Given that their self-expression is quite subtle, truly knowing a Water sign often involves a long but worthwhile learning process. Whether a nurturing Cancerian, intense Scorpio or an empathetic Piscean, Water signs are complex, deep, introspective and anything but frivolous. While Water types can be moody, changeable, over-sensitive and irritable, they can also be affectionate, playful, humorous and loyal.

The Water element is connection-seeking, fluid, and paradoxically powerful yet powerless, representing the strongest and weakest traits of the human experience, moves around obstacles, is chaotic by nature, has a sense of oneness, is life-giving and life-sustaining, purifying, rebirthing, feels 'in the moment', is wise and understanding on deeper levels, is boundless, aroused by empathy and passion, is never the same, feels others' feelings, can be a curse or a blessing, absorbs feelings and can lose itself in its response, can operate out of others' feelings, is generally unconditional, is creative, past-dwelling, nurturing, sensuous, surrendering and sacrificing, has depth of self, has emotional integrity, contains itself or allows its feelings to gush forth depending on the situation, can idealise suffering, shies from the mundane world, is relentless, eroding, nostalgic and sentimental, and has a great capacity for depth in union. Watery temperaments have an innate capacity for sympathy, protectiveness, romance, empathy, intuition, psychic insights and sensitivity, but can be subject to secrecy, and can suffer mysterious, unfathomable moods. They can also be hidden, escapist, evasive, dependent, manipulative, 'slippery' and elusive.

The Water element puts a strong emphasis on relationships and they are compassionate and responsive to others' needs, especially if Cancer or Pisces predominate. Scorpio is a little less subtle than the other two, being ruled by Pluto and having a tendency towards more hidden, penetrative and occasionally explosive behaviour; passion and intensity are also Scorpio traits which the other two express much more gently.

Overall, Water is the cleansing, purifying element, necessary for all life. It is the major component of the human body and is associated with our lymph systems. In the form of rain, it nourishes the Earth, promoting and enabling fertility and growth. Water is formless and meandering, and it connects, enters and merges, while still retaining its own essence. It needs the freedom to flow and like the tides, it has its own behaviours and rhythms. Sensitive to stimuli, it is highly receptive, absorbing that which comes into contact with it, and often encompasses or envelopes those things.

Self-contained and protective, Watery types are able to experience the contentment of simply being, continually replenishing themselves from their inner reservoirs. These types are flowing, and oriented towards forming connections and blending with their surroundings. Highly instinctive and feeling, they are attuned to unseen realms, and possess a psychic sensitivity which enables them to excel at nonverbal communication and to hear and receive unspoken emotions. They are also imaginative, dedicated to their ideals, introspective and creative. Although some Watery types may not consider themselves religious, they have a heightened sensitivity to spiritual disciplines and forces, and so are naturally drawn to these areas by their very natures.

Water is encouraged to experience emotions without repressing or being overwhelmed by them, achieve inner emotional security, and to handle intuitive and psychic sensitivities adeptly, that is, without becoming engulfed by them and through being both open and self-protective.

Positive Water Qualities ★ Empathic, feeling-oriented, flexible, compassionate, sensitive, responsive, deep, intuitive, receptive, nurturing, adaptable, caring, devoted, self-contained, retentive, protective, attuned to the unseen, imaginative, private, introspective, idealistic, flowing, understanding, resourceful, spiritual, psychically aware

Negative Water Qualities ★ Secretive, wallowing, evasive, closed, cynical, overly subjective, brooding, self-absorbed, oversensitive, disillusioned, elusive, overly emotional, passive, waterlogged, clingy to past, moody, gullible, self-pitying, overwhelmed, inaccessible, hidden, manipulative, resigned, withholding, timid, expect too much, irrational, muddled thinking, directionless, devitalised by fears which focus on negatives, takes everything personally, blaming, indecisive, insecure, vindictive, unrealistic, confused, dependent/co-dependent, symbiotic, compulsive, drifting, regressive, impressionable

THE ARCHANGEL OF WATER ★ GABRIEL

An archangel is an angel of greater than ordinary rank. They possess a stronger, more powerful essence than the guardian angels, through overseeing and guiding the other angels who are said to be with us here on Earth. The word 'angel' derives from the Greek word *angelos* meaning 'messenger'. To humans, angels are often seen as bringers as all sorts of messages. Angels in all their forms are believed to bring the message of 'spirit' into matter, carrying the blueprints of creation and the Source from the Divine into the manifest world. Angels are not and never have been human; they, like fairies and nature spirits, are part of a different evolutionary pattern – but they do appear to us in human form (usually with wings) because that is what we understand. An angel can be in many different places at once, and with the same intensity and concentration, and wish for us to be aware of them and benefit from them.

There are said to be three categories of angels in the cosmos, each with three subdivisions *. 'Angel' is the generic term and also relates specifically to those closest to the physical. Similarly, archangel may be taken to mean any of the higher orders, and indeed signifies the order just above ordinary 'angel'. Found in a number of religious traditions, the word 'archangel' itself is usually associated with the Abrahamic religions. The word archangel is of Greek origin, and means literally 'chief angel'. All archangels end with the 'el' suffix, 'el' meaning 'in God' and the first part of the name meaning what each individual Angel specialises in. The archangel who rules your sign will be the one with whom you most resonate.

The astrological sign is an energy signature, a matrix of a specific stellar pattern that will subtly affect and influence you. Although there are many associations for the great archangels of the Universe, we must keep in mind there is great overlapping in their duties and guidance. For example, we may say that one is for healing and another for protection, but they can all perform the functions of the others, and each has only areas of greater focus and responsibilities. Four of the multitude of archangelic beings work intimately with the Earth. These are Raphael (Air), Michael (Fire), Gabriel (Water) and Uriel (Earth). Associated with each of these archangels are one of the four elements, specific colours, one of the four directions or quarters of the Earth, three signs of the zodiac, and a variety of other energies and powers. Understanding these associations and considering them in relation to our own paths, can help us determine with which of them we are more likely to resonate. Your sign, being of the Water element, vibrates to the essence of Gabriel.

* The first sphere, the *Heavenly Counsellors*, comprises Seraphim, Cherubim and Thrones. The second sphere, the *Heavenly Governors*, comprises Dominions, Virtues and Powers. The third sphere, the *Heavenly Messengers*, comprises Principalities, Archangels and Angels. Of course, all such classifications are a human construct, a way of placing order upon the unknowable and allowing us to perceive something about which we have no words to express. However, as long as we think of angelic hierarchies as a way of working with celestials, of remembering important attributes, and we are able to imagine and experience these beings, this order of angels will prove useful to those wishing to draw upon their messages and assistance.

★ ARCHANGEL GABRIEL'S ASSOCIATIONS ★

Element of Water
The Western quarter of the Earth

The winter season
The colours emerald, silver and sea green
The crystals opal, fluorite and moonstone
The astrological signs of Cancer, Scorpio and Pisces

Gabriel, meaning "Strength of God" or "The Divine is my strength," is known as the messenger and can help us to find our true soul's purpose. As archangel of the Moon and ruler of dreams, Gabriel is chief archangel of the night and the alter ego of Michael, the Sun archangel. Some consider Gabriel a feminine energy. The archangel of life, hope, truth, astral travel, unconscious wisdom, illumination and love, he inspires and motivates artists and communicators, and delivers important prophetic messages to people. He guards the sacred places of the world and the sacred waters of life. Gabriel provides intuitive teaching, guidance, mystical experiences, inspiration and enlightenment of spiritual duties, including awakening within us a greater understanding of dreams. He can be called upon when you are feeling alone, afraid or vulnerable. Gabriel is said to be the angel who chooses the souls to be born and cares for them in the womb. He is also an angel of death, but a gentle one, bringing release from sorrow and pain.

CANCER'S ZODIAC ARCHANGEL ★ GABRIEL

Additionally, each sign is associated with a particular archangel. Such knowledge can help you to build up a relationship with these beings, based upon your strengths and needs. However, no link is rigid, and as you work with angels you will come to develop your own affinities. When invoking a specific archangel, a useful ritual to draw them closer is to light a candle in that angel's colour, burn some oil or incense of its scent, and hold the appropriate crystal while focusing on what you are needing guidance on.

YOUR ARCHANGEL ★ Please see previous information under the heading 'Archangel Gabriel's Associations'.

SCENT/OIL ★ Jasmine

CANDLE COLOUR ★ Orange-gold

CRYSTAL ★ Moonstone or beryl

THE DEVIC REALMS & WATER ★ WEST: REALM OF THE UNDINES

"Through magick we do conjure the Elements, evoking unto us the special properties of the Life-force for our learning and our coming-into-light. And yet are there secret paths of knowledge that have fallen from the minds of men … For the way of Magick is a path to sacred knowledge, of reverence and humility - and the world is a wondrous place. Yet how many amongst us have fathomed these depths?"
***Merlin's Book of Magick and Enchantment*, Nevill Drury**

Deva is a Sanskrit word that means 'shining one'. Devas are the life force within nature, and there are four devic realms - Fire, Earth, Air and Water - which contain ethereal elemental spirits or sprites. Elementals are the building blocks of nature, and close to being true energy and consciousness. The four elements correspond to four different states of matter: energy/transmutation (Fire), gas (Air), liquid (Water) and solid (Earth), which are linked to the four human states of consciousness: inspiration, thought, feeling and practicality. There are four spirits, or elementals, which reside in the devic realms, associated with each element. People have been painting pictures, telling stories and writing about these devic realms for hundreds of years, albeit sometimes through disguised mediums such as fairytales or children's fantasy stories like Tolkien's *Lord of the Rings*. The power of the natural world is easily observed and since ancient times primal forces have been ascribed to various spirit beings. Belief in nature spirits is of such ancient origin and is Universal; cultures everywhere have names or words to describe them. In the sixteenth century, a famous Swiss physician, alchemist and mystic called Paracelsus * defined these beings as 'Elementals', classifying them according to the element of nature they inhabit. There are four main levels of elemental beings: Gnomes (Earth), Undines (Water), Sylphs (Air), and Salamanders (Fire). The fifth element of Ether is the element from which came forth the other four, and Ether, or Spirit, has never been defined in any particular category, and encompasses the aspects and beings of all the other elements.

Elementals are usually benevolent guardian beings or spirits that look after nature's secrets and treasures in whatever part of the natural realm they occupy. They can only be seen or 'felt' by those possessing heightened psychic abilities, yet they can be summoned by those practising alchemy, spells and magic in order to harness the forces of nature for their own particular intentions. In our modern lives, it may seem as though this magic doesn't exist, but the truth is that most of us are simply less in touch with it than ever before. The consequence of this is that we are destroying vast areas of land, polluting waters, creating toxic landscapes, and disrespecting the laws of nature, which often whisper their messages softly. It is therefore important for us to look at the beauty that surrounds us with true appreciation and genuine regard, and to open ourselves up to the magic resides within it. The four devic realms can teach us much about nature; they act as custodians for the four elements, and learning to work with them is a way of attuning to all the energies and beings of nature. Elementals are four-dimensional, and have nothing to obstruct their movements. Therefore, they move as easily through matter as we do through air and space. They do require some contact with humans for their own evolution. Helping to direct them is an overseer, traditionally called the King of that element, and an archangel. Each of these elements is affiliated with one of the four directions and each elemental spirit embodies its own special energy. If you wish to re-connect and re-harmonise yourself by working with nature and its messages and lessons, you could begin by learning a little about your element's realm: Your element is Water, which is connected with the West direction and the realm of the Undines.

* Paracelsus is considered the most original medical thinker of the sixteenth century. His belief in supernatural beings, intuition and the invisible causes of illness helped him discover hydrogen and nitrogen. Paracelsus believed that "Elementals are unlike pure spirits for they are mortal, but they are not like man for they have no soul."

★ UNDINES ★

Undine is from the Latin *unda*, meaning 'wave', and therefore these spirits are said to control the waters of the Earth. Undines are perhaps the best known of the four elementals as they appear frequently in stories and legends. Usually female nymph-like beings, they are beautiful, eager to tempt, and enjoy associating with humans. They like to lure with their musical enchantments, creating sweet, intoxicating melodies with their harps, or singing pure, uplifting songs for those who are still and near enough to listen. Found wherever there is a natural source of water, the undines are responsible for the vitality within liquids and they also work with plants that grow underwater. All water upon our planet - rain, rivers, oceans, lakes, et cetera - has immense undine activity. Undines, like the gnomes, are subject to mortality, but they are more enduring. They are dependent upon humans for growth, and as we evolve, so do they.

One of the most famous of the Water elementals is the Lady of the Lake who features in the legends of King Arthur. This undine beauty rose from her lake to present Arthur with the sword Excalibur and captured the hearts of many of the Knights of the Round Table. The undines govern the realm of autumn and Water, the west, and the Cups in the Tarot deck. In many religions, water symbolises the initiation through baptism in the 'waters of life'. In ancient times all great rivers were considered holy and sacred, without which nothing could prosper; springs, wells, ponds, pools and fountains were regarded as holy places where great healing properties and energies could be found and prophecies foretold.

The Undines work to maintain the astral body of humans and to stimulate our feeling nature. This is associated with heightened psychic functions as well as emotional ones. Theirs is an energy of intuition, creation and birth. Undines guard and carry the secrets of the Dreamtime, inner visions, emotions, feelings and journeys.

Water is the springwell of life, and these beings are essential to our finding that springwell within. Essential to the gifts of healing, purification and empathy, they work with humans to help us discover both our inner and outer beauty. Human beings are made of around 75 per cent water, which acts as a channel or stream for all physical and chemical changes to occur; and the same percentage again is echoed by our planet's water composition - three quarters of the Earth's surface is covered by seas, rivers and oceans, which are governed by the Moon, which provides a natural rhythmical rulership over planetary phenomena. Folklore says that water gives to us what we give to it. The undines, who dwell in the Watery realms, will indeed do the same. The King of Water is Llyr or Niksa, its archangel is Gabriel, its magickal tool is the Cup (which calls down the spirits into form), and its sacred ceremonial stones are Amethyst, Moonstone and Pearl.

INVOKING THE WATER DEVAS

Water represents flow and change – in many myths crossing a stream signifies a shift in consciousness, all cultures regard water as the biggest life-giving source, and baptism is a rite of passage in some religions. Water is mysterious, moody and changeable. Water devas embody all of these attributes and most are hauntingly beautiful. Water can be a tricky medium to work with, but overall they help to connect you with the wellsprings of your feelings, bringing sympathy, empathy and the bonds of human love. If you are feeling raw, lonely, sad, uncared for or buffeted by life, ask the water devas for their help. Undines will give you blessings when you are going into any situation that requires deep emotional strength. They can be found in any body of water, the tides and rains, in mists and in fogs, and are purifying, healing and cleansing.

THE WEST DIRECTION'S CORRESPONDENCES

If you wish to work more with your particular element and direction, the following may help propel your wishes and magical journey:

Time of Day ★ Sunset
Polarity ★ Female, negative
Exhortation ★ *To know*
Musical Instruments ★ Strings, bells
Colours ★ Blue, green
Season ★ Autumn
Magical Instrument ★ Cup
Altar Symbol ★ Chalice
Communion Symbol ★ Wine, Water
Archangel ★ Gabriel
Human Sense ★ Taste
Art Forms ★ Music, song
Animals ★ Fish, whales
Mythical Beast ★ Sea serpent
Magical Arts ★ Healing
Guide Forms ★ Moon, Water goddess
Meditation ★ The ocean, rivers
Images & Themes ★ Lakes, pools, living underwater, healing, calm, the setting Sun

HOW YOU CAN GET IN TOUCH WITH YOUR WATER ENERGY

"Water flows on and on ... It does not shrink from any dangerous spot nor from any plunge, and nothing can make it lose its own essential nature. It remains true to itself under all conditions."
I Ching, hexagram 29, k'an/k'an

★ Use Water energy when making wishes around the following: Healing, spiritual and psychic development, relationship harmony, emotional issues, psychosomatic illnesses, dreams, trust and faith.

★ Spend time in and around water - oceans, rivers, streams, lakes, waterfalls.

★ Carry a small spray bottle of water with you and spritz yourself with it throughout the day.

★ Float in the water - surrender to its unerring support and let it keep you afloat.

★ Research, make and use gem (crystal) essences.

★ Try to take a bath rather than a shower; you can linger for longer, and even meditate more effectively, in a still bath.

★ Engage in water sports (not too extreme though, unless Scorpio is strong in your chart!), such as water skiing, swimming, kayaking, surfing, yachting, scuba diving, canoeing, sailing, or water volleyball.

★ Drink lots of H2O!

★ Meditate on the Cups suit in the Tarot (the Cups suit represents the Water element).

★ Eat watery, water-based foods, such as brothy soups, watermelon and juicy fruits.

★ Purify and cleanse your body occasionally, by undertaking a day-long fast / liquid diet.

★ Sleep on a waterbed.

★ Green-coloured crystals will activate your connection with the element of Water and enhance hope, healing, love and creativity.

★ Join an emotional support group - or facilitate one.

★ Install a water fountain in your home, garden or office - water features, placed strategically, are believed in Feng Shui tradition to attract certain desired things into your environment and experience.

★ Wear and surround yourself with the colours blue, silver and green.

★ Decorate your home or office with soothing watery images, such as scenic lakes, panoramic beach photographs, ocean-side postcards, and themed paintings.

★ Listen and meditate to ocean waves and bubbling brook sounds on an audio system.

★ Walk in the rain, jump in puddles.

★ Visit a spa regularly, and indulge in saunas and Jacuzzis - better still, install one in your home!

★ Learn and practice graceful, flowing forms of movement, such as t'ai chi.

★ Express your emotions fearlessly; try to use them as your ally.

★ Nurture others and inspire them to nurture themselves.

★ Express your feelings through art, poetry and drama.

★ Cultivate a spiritual practice.

★ Develop your counselling and listening skills so you can help others - and yourself!

★ Meditate regularly. Embrace your inner silence, peace and spiritual essence.

★ When working with the Water element in magical rituals, stand at the West quarter of your special space, as the West is its domain, and invite its living essence into your 'circle'.

★ Use chalices, bowls, crystals, blue or silver items, and cauldrons to represent your element. If you are fortunate enough to live near the ocean, its tides can be a great energising force that evokes dramatic magical transformations. When the tide goes out, visualise your worries being drawn away. High tide is an optimum time to focus on wish magic, and as the waves move in closer, imagine your dreams coming towards you. Spells cast on a riverbank or near a spring will also be empowered by the moving energy of Water.

★ The best days on which to employ Water magic are Monday, ruled by the Moon, and Friday, ruled by the planet of love Venus.

★ Water spirits are also known as sea nymphs, naiads, undines or sprites. They are responsible for the cleansing, refreshing and clearing of our spirits, so Water signs would be wise to adopt one (or all) of these as their very own spirit guide!

YOUR MODE ★ CARDINAL

Each sign belongs to one of the three quadruplicities, Cardinal, Fixed and Mutable. If we closely examine the Earth's yearly cycle, we can form a very accurate picture of the nature of these quadruplicities, for they correspond directly with the manifestation of the seasons. Each season has three months: the first month brings the new phase of the cycle, the second month brings a concentration of the season's energy to its fullest expression, and the third month represents the transition from the current season to the next one. The astrological quadruplicities represent the three basic qualities in all life: creation (Cardinal), perseveration (Fixed) and destruction (Mutable). Every thing that is born, from a period of time to a human being, experiences a life and then dies. In this context, death can be taken to mean that the form of the energy changes; but the energy itself can never be annihilated, for form is mortal, whereas essence is immortal.

The Cardinal mode covers the signs Aries, Cancer, Libra and Capricorn, and is the most initiating and self-motivated group of the three modes, able to instigate and inspire beginnings; in other words, to "get the ball rolling." The Cardinal mode has an initiating action and quality, operating with ambition, enthusiasm, independence and enterprise. Forceful, opportunistic, and at times aggressive, you have the will to accomplish and creatively project yourself onto the world. You charge right in to get the job done - but you can fail just as spectacularly. Although you have a great start-up ability, tenacity and endurance are not your fortes, and you often don't follow things through to the end.

If there is no crisis for you to tackle, you may even make one up just to create a challenge for yourself. You find it hard to be held under anyone's thumb and will always find a way to wriggle free to set off on your next quest. Your energies may be directed towards yourself, your home and family, or the wider world of career or society, but in any case it is difficult to divert your attention away from your chosen course. Cardinal signs have great drive, are self-motivated and would rather lead than follow. It is hard to influence you because you make your own firm decisions and believe that you know best. The Cardinal mode signifies beginnings, decision-making, boldness, courage, will, new starts, and initiations. You tend to be dynamic, authorative, 'bossy', active, restless, involved, busy and energetic, and are determined initiators of goals and new purposes. The Sun's entry into the Cardinal signs indicates the beginning of seasons in the northern hemisphere: the start of Aries marks the Spring Equinox, the beginning of Libra the Autumn Equinox, the start of Cancer the Winter Solstice, and the beginning of Capricorn the Summer Solstice.

Cancer is the most sensitive of the Cardinal quality; you are emotionally assertive and even though you appear timid and reserved, you know what you want and how to go about getting it.

YOUR RULING PLANET ★ THE MOON

The Subconscious Soul

Planetary Meditation
I am my Earth (my body),
and my Sky (my transcendence)
I am my Sun (my spirit),
and my Moon (my soul)
I am my Venus (my pleasure),
and my Jupiter (my faith)
I am my Mars (my courage),
and my Saturn (my lessons)
I am my Mercury (my thoughts),
and my Uranus (my truth)
I am my Neptune (my dreams),
and my Pluto (my transformation)

Each planet has its own distinctive and original meaning which, according to its position in the zodiac, combines with the qualities that are inherent in each of the twelve astrological signs. If a planet is your sign's ruler, however, it exerts a significant influence upon your life, regardless of its birth chart or zodiacal position.

Luminary ★ Associated with the Subconscious, Instincts, Intuition, Habits, Fluctuations, Emotions, Feelings ★ 27.3 Day Cycle

★ KEY WORDS ★

Childhood, the Past, Memory, Emotions, Feelings, the Subconscious, Instincts, Habits, Mothering, the Mother, Habitual and Instinctive Responses, Fluctuations, Nurturing, Empathy, Soul, the Inner Personality, Receptivity, Moods, Security

★ KEY CONCEPTS ★

★ Attachments to the Past ★
★ Memory & Subconscious ★
★ Emotions & Feelings ★
★ Ancestral Inheritance ★
★ The Soul ★
★ Impressionability ★
★ Domesticity ★
★ The Childhood Experience ★
★ The Mother or Mother Figure ★
★ Receptivity & Magnetism ★

Day ★ Monday

Number ★ 2

Basic Energy & Magic ★ Emotions, Intuition

Colours ★ Silver, Pastel Shades, White, Blue, Cream, Silvery Grey, Opalescent & Iridescent Hues

Gods/Goddesses/Angel ★ Artemis, Luna, Gabriel, Selene, Diana, Hecarte, Isis

Metals ★ Silver, Aluminium

Gems/Minerals ★ Moonstone, Opal, Pearl, Selenite, Angelite, Celestite

Trees/Shrubs ★ Willow, Hawthorn, Silver Birch, Lemon, Eucalyptus, Sycamore, Tamarind, Maple, Alder

Flowers/Herbs ★ Convolvulus, Watercress, Myrrh, Poppy, Jasmine, Lotus, Clary Sage, Rosewood, Wintergreen, Ylang Ylang, Mimosa, Freesia, Chamomile, Gardenia, Lemon Balm, Lily

Wood ★ Birch

Fabric ★ Silk

Animals ★ Crab, Owl

Element ★ Water

Zodiacal Sign ★ Cancer

Zodiacal Influences ★ Rules Cancer; Exalted in Taurus; Detriment Capricorn; Fall Scorpio

Although not a planet, the Moon is our nearest celestial neighbour and exerts a great influence upon the Earth and all life that dwells upon it. The gravitational pull of the Moon affects our bodily fluids, which contribute to about ninety per cent of our biological make-up. Taking an average of 27.3 * days to pass through all of the twelve zodiac signs, it stays in each for around 2.5 days.

People with a strong Moon placement, and those ruled by this powerful sphere, such as Cancer, in their natal chart can be moody, irrational, changeable, over-reactive, insecure, emotional and clingy.

The symbol for the Moon ☽ is a representation of its crescent in its waxing phase from New to Full, but it can also be seen as two half circles - these form a bowl shape, a receptacle, a feminine container that 'receives' and 'holds' anything put into it. The half circle, unlike the full circle of the Sun, is finite and incomplete, almost as if striving for wholeness. The crescent symbol for the Moon was chosen by the ancient astrologers to represent a person's soul, complementing the Sun's symbolism of one's spirit or *outer* manifestation of character.

The Moon and our emotional nature go hand in hand. It influences the type of nurturing we need from our mothers to make us complete, well-rounded people. It describes our symbolic womb, where and how we seek comfort and feel safe. It also influences how we relate to others, our emotional responses, moods, changes, fluctuations and our instinctual 'knowing'.

The Moon, Earth's satellite, is about a quarter of the size of our planet, and its light is merely a reflection of sunlight, it gives back only seven per cent of the light it receives. It is around five billion years old, as estimated by the study of Lunar dust. Although the Moon is Earth's satellite, the Sun's pull on it is far greater; indeed, the Sun is the common centre of gravity for both bodies. The Moon has four basic phases in its cycle: The New Moon, the First

Quarter, Full Moon and the Last Quarter. It is known by scientists that plant growth is affected by the Moon, that the tidal rhythms depend upon her movements, and that the female menstrual cycle corresponds to the sidereal Lunar month.

In mythology, the Moon is personified as the goddess Luna, Selene, Artemis or Diana. In the Tarot deck, The Moon - card number 18 of the Major Arcana - reminds us that, like the Moon, some things can be hidden from view and we may not always be able to see the full picture.

Astrologically, the Moon's influence is cold, moist, fruitful and feminine, and because its visual image alters constantly, it characterises changeability. Consequently, its influence is often unsettling, and those with a prominent Moon in their horoscope, such as someone with a Cancer Sun, Moon or Ascendant, will likely be emotionally sensitive.

The Moon has two major cycles: the sidereal period (its relation to the stars), the 27 days, 7 hours, and 43 minutes it takes to make a complete revolution through the constellations of the zodiac; and the synodic period, the 29 days, 12 hours and 44 minutes of time between one New Moon and the next one, completing one Lunar cycle in a slightly longer period than the first. The synodic period is commonly called the Lunar month. The Moon is said to be waxing when the New Moon moves from New to Full, and as the Moon moves away from the Full Moon and back to the New Moon, it is said to be waning.

The Moon in the birth chart is very important, second only or arguably even equal to the Sun in its cosmic influence, because it is thought to reflect the true character of one's soul and thus forms an integral part of the personality. In fact, throughout most of human history, the Moon has been of more symbolic importance than the Sun, but in many cultures still, it is this Lunar influence which plays a larger role in chart interpretation. The Moon has long been worshipped under a multiplicity of names, and there is hardly a goddess in the entire pantheon of the Greeks or Celts who does not possess a Lunar aspect or manifestation of some kind.

The Moon governs that inner part of ourselves that can only be seen when someone knows us well. In many ways it is hidden for the most part, and must be drawn out. Your Lunar side reveals how you deal with feelings, how you handle relationships, how you respond emotionally to experiences with others, and how you react to other people unconsciously. Often the Moon reflects a great deal more about a person than any other planet, particularly in regard to their interpersonal relationships. It could even be regarded as the archetypal mirror, reflecting back to us our true self. But it has an outer expression also, and not only reveals our own inner motivations and security needs, but the style in which we seek to comfort and nurture others.

The Moon is essentially receptive and passive; it reflects the life experience rather than initiating it. Fluctuating and cyclical, the Moon is the planet (although technically a satellite) of feelings, emotions, habits, the subconscious, and instinctual reactions.

The glyph (or symbol) for the Moon is the crescent, which is the symbol selected by the ancient astrologers to express a person's soul. The crescent symbol could also be seen as standing for the womb, container of life. (It is also a visual representation of the shape of the waxing Moon). Functioning primarily as a receptacle, it can be said that everything we experience is funnelled into the womb of the Moon. Everything we remember, everything we have experienced and felt, is stored in this bubbling cauldron. Some esoteric astrologers label the Moon the 'planet of past karma', another way of describing it as a limitless well of feeling patterns which, for the most part, subconsciously directs our behaviours and actions in the present. And while the Sun symbol represents the infinite and unmanifested potential, the Moon symbol reveals the finite and manifested, or that which already exists, and that we carry on our journey as a genetically-gifted ancestral imprint or memory. As the Moon signifies the past and rules all life-giving and life-sustaining liquids *, it follows that in the fluids of brain and body, it accumulates and carries forward our personal evolutionary history. Once it is understood that Water signifies the emotions in the language of mythology, it becomes clear how both our individual moods and our collective cultural, inherited attachments are strongly influenced by it.

While the Sun signifies our individuality, the Moon describes our personality, and in a horoscope it is imperative that the Sun and Moon are in harmonious aspect so that the will of the individuality and the feelings of the personality can be integrated and expressed in a sound, balanced manner. A disharmonious relationship between these two luminaries does not mean that an individual will not be successful, but it will almost always indicate difficulties and conflicts when learning to balance the will and the emotions.

As an indicator of domestic and home life, the Moon can tell us about our love or feelings towards our family, as well as the style of our property and residence.

The Moon is the repository of memories. As your ruling planet, Cancerians often dwell in the past and may spend much of their time longing for the past, finding it difficult to move forward. The Moon strongly represents what has gone before, and those whose ruling planet is the Moon, often carry forward underlying moods and attitudes from this time.

The Moon represents your inner world and its energy can be most effectively utilised by nurturing yourself and others; this will vary depending on the element of your Moon sign. Relating to others on an emotional plane can be a great gift, as empathy comes naturally to the Moon. Intuition is also emphasised and should be developed to its fullest potential for you to truly shine and excel. However, a tendency to be over-sensitive, introverted or reactive can also occur.

The Moon is the innermost core of our being, our private feelings, and subconscious habits. It is the caring, nurturing sustainer of life, the 'mother' of the zodiac. Representing the infancy stage of the lifespan, as well as the mother and any other matriarchal influences that leave a deep impression on the psyche, it informs us of our earliest, unconscious memories. It tells us about how we seek security, our urge to nurture, and our nurturing style. It describes our childhood experience, our receptivity, individual fluctuations and cycles.

As the Moon is oriented to survival and security, its pull in a person's horoscope can be stronger than that of the Sun. And where the Sun acts, the Moon *reacts*. Because it carries the energy of ingrained habits and the instinctual behaviours we express without conscious thought, it seems to flow more naturally than any of the other planetary forces. But the Moon has a metaphorical dark side as well, for we may continue to dwell within the frame of reference we set for ourselves in our childhood, repeating the same behaviours and thoughts until they form deep habitual patterns and entrapping ruts which we may find difficult to climb out from. Contrary to popular belief, and the fact that the word 'lunatic' has its origins in the Latin *luna* meaning 'Moon' (arising from the belief that changes in the Lunar cycles caused intermittent insanity), the Moon does not always mean madness - far from it - but it can help to show where any psychological blocks lie.

The Moon is the primary feminine principle in the birth chart, and offers insights into the quintessential feminine archetype. As such, it rules such female-leaning themes as emotions, mothering, maternal instincts, caring and nurturing. The Moon also represents our mother or mother figure (your experience and expectations of your mother), and the feminine side of ourselves, indicating how strongly these manifest in an individual, male or female. As the 'mother' of the zodiac, it reveals much about how we experienced our mother and to a large extent how we still do into adulthood. No matter what sign our physical mother was born under, the mother is experienced in a style characteristic of her child's Moon sign.

As the Moon is also about attachment, it stands for our first attachment figure, which was usually a primary parent (usually the mother, sometimes the father or another relative). It reveals how we seek security and how we respond if our security is threatened. With a strong feminine energy emanating from it, the Moon is also about our birth, fertility, containment, development of empathy, responses to the impressions we receive, unconditional love, bonding mechanisms, our intuitive functions, vulnerability, dependency, and is significantly a symbol of safety and our Inner Child.

As it represents what our childhood experience is likely to be, and childhood is essentially a time where our consciousness has not yet fully developed, our Moon sign traits seem to be more apparent in our younger years. We will usually show our Moon sign traits more so than our Sun sign traits during this developing period of infancy and early childhood, until we have the presence of mind to more consciously develop our ego and true core self (the Sun). While we move towards our Sun essence throughout our lives, the Moon begins operating at our conception, so it affects us in utero as well as after birth. The Moon holds the 'memories' of our in utero experience and as such we can 'feel' these memories. It can even show whether our in utero experience was positive or not.

The Moon, affecting our childhood so much, also plays an indirect role in our adult relationships. It reveals whether or not and how our emotional needs were met during this crucial stage of life development, and how this will be replayed and carried into our adult relations. For many of us, grown-up relationships are driven by an unconscious quest to get those earlier, unfulfilled needs met, or we may put up a barrier to resist being overwhelmed by another person's needs.

The fact that we journey figuratively towards the symbolism of our Sun sign as we grow older, is perhaps a way of saying that beyond childhood, we must learn to detach ourselves from purely instinctive reactions and link ourselves more strongly and directly with the conscious sense of purpose and destiny that our Sun sign has set out for us. In other words, emotional thought patterning from our pasts must be overcome or transcended in order to fulfil our Solar destiny, particularly in the West where Solar-inspired qualities such as ambition, extroversion, accomplishment and action are paramount and equate to conventional success and achievement.

The earliest calendars were in fact Lunar, and had these stayed in effect, we would have thirteen months of 28.5 days each. A standard year is composed of thirteen Lunar months. As the complete sequence of Moon phases from New to Full takes a little over 29 days, some years will have twelve Full Moons, while others will have thirteen, meaning that one month will occasionally have two Moons; this second Full Moon in a calendar month is known as the legendary 'Blue Moon' and happens roughly once every two-and-a-half years. It is believed that any magic performed under a Blue Moon is more powerful than normal.

It was patriarchal culture ** that deleted the thirteenth month, contrived the Solar calendar we use today, and put an aura of bad luck around the number thirteen. The Lunar calendar gave us knowledge of natural cycles, for many creatures and plants follow the ebb and flow of the Lunar sphere. Tides, animal behaviour, plant growth and human cognitive functions are all affected by the phases of the Moon. Knowledge of this cycle was a momentous first step to understanding the structure of time, helping humankind take steps towards some mastery of their environment and its often challenging conditions.

After knowledge of the Lunar cycle came knowledge of the Solar cycle, with the Sun-Moon relationship being able to be measured by noting the changing proportions of day and night. This knowledge is what marks out the equinoxes and solstices. Observing the Solar cycles enclosed the Lunar cycle into a longer, 365 day calendar. The calendar we use today, the Gregorian calendar, is based on the Solar cycle, but is disconnected from the year's natural 'cross' formed by the solstices and equinoxes. Further, the Gregorian calendar indicates no resonance with the Lunar cycle. The natural world, however, continues to be influenced and moved by the Moon's cycles.

While the Sun symbolises our essence and spirit, the Moon represents our *soul*, and is the expression of our sensitive inner self. Through the five physical senses, we become aware of the world around us, and we then perceive and interpret this in our own way. So, the image we create of ourselves and the world around us is, in fact, the fruit of our imagination - which is a realm of the Moon. The Moon will travel any distance through time and space to find what you want; she will dip freely into the limitless ocean of the collective subconscious to bring it to you. It is vital to recognise, however, that the Moon will obey a veiled hint even more readily than a direct command, because this is apt to be a more accurate reflection of your real *need* than the wish you have consciously expressed.

Because food is a basic need, the Moon can also be connected with our eating patterns and food habits. As well as nourishing the physical body, its placement and sign describes what spiritual, mental and emotional 'fuel' a person needs to nurture their soul, and also shows the ability to nurture ourselves through eating and 'feeding' ourselves.

Concepts and words associated with the Moon are changeability, Monday, fertility, lakes, emotions, family, moods, women, chickens, harbours, fish, sailing, drains, collecting, markets, ferries, smooth, abdomen, subconscious, herbs, aquatic matters, houses, laundry, domestic front, babies, drinks, fecundity, mammals, baking, wife, barmaids, eggs, glass, melons, beverages, milk, fruitful, rooms, kitchens, habits, wells, boathouses, soft, linen, streams, fickle, breasts, eyes, hydro, inconsistent, bottles, brooks, cafes, familiar, white, inns, canals, lilies, feelings, caterers, home, maternal, houseboats, meals, common, rivers, cooking, fluids, cows, crescents, flabby, crops, cupboards, dairies, plumbing, liquids, damp, glands, dew, wet, poultry, seafood, gardens, stomach, teardrops, housewives, humid, digestion, fountains, dining, infants, docks, lunacy, nurseries, pantries, maternity, timidity, oysters, menstruation, moonstones, night, mother, planting, mushrooms, residences, swimming, taverns, midwives, pools, ports, water, moats, nourishment, pale, pearls, pipes, public, receptive, marshes, barges, instincts, sentimental, irrigation, childhood, children, females, baths, cleaning, tides, impressionable, restaurants, washing and silver. I'm sure you get the idea!

Overall, the strength or weakness of the Moon's natal position is most important in the determination of your personal magnetism, general sympathies, imagination and sometimes unknowable inner landscape. The Apollo astronauts who landed on the Moon in 1969 collected samples which, scientists later concluded, posed more questions about Lunar origins than they answered. Those who returned from that iconic mission spoke of a profoundly affecting spiritual experience which ultimately changed many of their life directions. And so the Moon remains shrouded in mystery, a keeper of sacred mysteries - just as our inner soul is, too.

This Lunar energy and influence, throughout your whole life, gives Cancerians the gifts of sensitivity, adaptability, sympathy, receptivity, empathy and imagination. Too much of this Lunar energy can make one dependent, clingy, moody, prone to martyrdom, neurotic, withdrawn, inconsistent, and lacking in leadership and courage. But the Cancerian always listens to the quiet whispers of her inner Lunar self, and trusts her heart and follows her intuition: after all, your motto is "I Feel," because deep down, you really do *feel* your and intuit way through life, your face always turned towards light of the Sun. How will *you* use your phenomenally powerful Lunar influence?

* The Moon rules the digestive juices, the glandular secretions of the lymphatic system, the stomach, breasts, ovaries and the sympathetic nervous system. The last is intimately associated with reactive behavioural patterns, emotions, affections and desires. Hence the origin of the term lunacy to describe severe emotional disturbances.

** Oddly enough, the only culture in the modern world to retain a Lunar calendar is arguably the most patriarchal of all - Islam, which is symbolised by the crescent Moon.

★ A NOTE ON ISIS, MOON GODDESS OF ENCHANTMENT ★

For thousands of years, perhaps the most significant goddess for Lunar magic has been the ancient Egyptian Isis. Goddess of the Moon and sea, she was often depicted wearing a crown that represented the Full Moon, held within the crescents of the Waxing and Waning Moons. Though she was one of the great goddesses of Egypt, worship of Isis became just as prevalent in the Greek and Roman cultures, particularly among females. Her cult spread throughout Europe and England, but Paris seemed to be Isis's special city (one school of thought believes that the name is a variation of Par-Isis, By Isis). Isis was named Lady of Lunar Enchantment in the novels of twentieth century occultist Dion Fortune. In today's world, she remains a central deity in goddess-focused organisations. Isis the Lunar goddess will connect you with magic and the deep feminine mysteries, the joys and trials of caring for others, being dedicated, and overcoming any difficulties with serenity and dignity.

YOUR HOUSE IN THE HOROSCOPE ★ THE FOURTH HOUSE

THE NADIR - IC - Cusp of the Fourth House. The IC is the degree of the zodiac directly below us at the moment of birth. The most private and deepest part of ourselves, it is the inner self: "My roots."

The Fourth House shows your home, both during childhood and in later life. It has a particular connection with the nurturing parent, not necessarily your biological mother, but whoever played that role for you. It also indicates our roots, origins, heritage and what we need in order to feel secure.

A house is one of the twelve sections dividing the terrestrial globe, viewed from a precise time and geographical place, into sectors from the poles to the horizon. The horoscope, or birth chart, is divided into these twelve sections called houses. Each house governs a different area or 'department' of life, such as relationships, career, leisure and even karma. The reason for this division of the Earth into houses can be understood when we consider that the Sun's rays affect us differently in the morning, at noon and at night, and also in summer and winter, and if we study the cause, we will readily observe that it is the angle at which the ray strikes us or the Earth which produces that difference in effect. Similarly, with the stellar rays, astrologers have observed that a child born at or near midday, when the Sun's rays strike the birthplace from the Tenth House, has an improved chance of public or career advancement in life than one born after sunset. By similar observations and tabulations, it has been found that the other planetary rays affect the various departments of life when their ray is projected through the other houses, and therefore each house is said to 'rule' or govern certain departments of the human life experience.

The Fourth House, ruled by Cancer, is the house of family, home, roots, heritage, origins and one's childhood experience. As it is an Angular House, the Fourth House is an extremely sensitive point. Any planet touching, or within 8 degrees of an angle, has an enhanced sphere of influence in your natal chart. As a Water sign, this is one of the three Houses of Soul or Endings, and, being an all-important Angular House, it forms one of the four significant angles of the birth chart (the other three being the First House or Ascendant, the Seventh House or Descendent, and the Tenth House or Midheaven). But where Scorpio is concerned with life on an interpersonal level and Pisces with life on a transpersonal, or Universal level, Cancer and the Fourth House are concerned with life on a personal level.

Traditionally the Fourth House is known as the House of Family and the Home, but it covers a wider and deeper range of concerns. Through the first three houses we have constructed a frame, now in the Fourth House we establish it and put down roots. The Fourth house tells us much about our origins, existential roots, psychological conditioning in early life, attitudes to our background, sense of belonging, and shows how we feel about the family unit and our home. It reveals the formative conditions in which our emotional growth took place, first during childhood - how and in which family, material, moral, cultural and social background one grew up - and about the way these roots unfolded in adulthood. The sign on its cusp will colour *how* we view our childhood home and family beginnings.

This house serves as a retreat, a haven to which you can return to restore yourself when the need arises, and provides a springboard, support or foundation for your very existence. It is the area of the horoscope where your roots grew, where and how you became an adult, and also the place to which you will come back once your part has been played and your destiny realised. In this way, it signifies both the beginning *and* the ending of the physical life experience. However, this return is not necessarily a pilgrimage to your childhood home, nor a regression; rather, it can be considered a return to one's self in its profound human and spiritual origins. Growth continues thereafter, but it can no longer be seen or measured with scientific instruments or methods.

So fundamentally, the Fourth House is about home and family. It rules your family circle and all matters concerning the domestic front, even including the building, block of land and everything in and around the house. This section gives indications about visitors, house guests, lodgers, intruders and others who call at your place, whether invited, uninvited, welcome or unwelcome. It also rules any additional property or real estate interests you have. Other exoteric and esoteric keywords include: private life, ancestry, family and relations, psychological foundations, biological inheritance, place of abode, the ashram and karma.

The Fourth House usually informs about the parents, the home environment and whether it is discordant or harmonious, as well as indicating what our conditions will be at the end of life, in old age, as life closes **. It tells us about the nature of our 'home base', how we feel secure, our sense of foundation, the influence of our family of origin, and the challenges of the home and how we deal or have dealt with them. It is connected with what we stand on, our foundations, the unconditional parent, and/or the parent who had the most influence, and significantly, from where we launch off into the more public arena when that time of life arrives.

The first level of this House deals with the basics: the physical home, emotional security and the mother. The second level reveals the development of emotional stability and feeling connected to the family roots. And the third level describes the integration of our emotional security as a foundation for our life (which projects straight up into the Tenth house, the house of career, public status and worldly achievements).

Overall, the Fourth House is strongly connected with the hearth, feeling at home, inner security, the parental home, the mother *, our experience of the mother or mother figure, the circumstances influencing childhood, our overall childhood experience, our early domestic life and environment, the nurturing parent, parents (especially the mother), hereditary factors, traditions, heritage, background, ancestors, emotional security and inherited patterns.

It represents conditions we are likely to encounter in the second half of life, after the age of 40, and tells us that maturity turns out to be much more fun than youth, for in our forties we have met most of life's challenges in the years before, survived them and established our life's principles and values.

* Please note that many astrologers link the Tenth house with the mother and the Fourth with the father, but it seems that this rule is variable. Some astrologers say that the parent who has the strongest influence is described in the Tenth house, others say the same sex parent is described in the Tenth house. Classically however, the Fourth house rules the mother (natural ruler Moon) and the Tenth house rules the father (natural ruler Saturn). It is also fitting that father or father figure matters are indicated in the Tenth house, as the father is usually (though not always) the conditional caregiver and Saturn is a conditional planetary energy. Although there is debate about whether the Fourth House is concerned with the mother or father - after all, the 'father' gives us our name and our 'genealogical line', or origins - there is no hard and fast rule, and your chart will have a way of telling you anyway.

** The concept of the home and the protective enclosing also has analogy with the womb and the grave - thus, the beginning and end of life are also concerns of this house.

YOUR OPPOSITE SIGN ★ CAPRICORN
WHAT YOU CAN LEARN FROM THE GOAT

If we look at the zodiac, we can see that it can be broadly divided into two hemispheres, this division being based on the natural division of the year by the two equinoxes. Astrologers often refer to the first six signs, the hemisphere in which the day predominates (the days being longer in the spring and summer months), as the Personal Sphere of Experience, and the second six signs, the hemisphere in which nights are longer, as the Social Sphere of Experience. These two halves of the zodiac perfectly balance and complement each other, and each individual 'personal' zodiac sign has something to teach its directly opposite 'social' zodiac sign. To generalise, the signs of the personal sphere tend to experience life through a type of self-projection and self-interest which is often socially uncomplicated, unsophisticated or naïve. Their objective is to learn greater social awareness and thereby integrate themselves with the larger, more Universal human collective. On the other hand, the signs of the social sphere are prone to experience life through the use of their more developed social consciousness. In essence, the personal signs (Aries, Taurus, Gemini, Cancer, Leo, Virgo) usually provide stimulation and new energy to their environment, while the social, more Universal signs (Libra, Scorpio, Sagittarius, Capricorn, Aquarius, Pisces) provide experience, opportunities for wider expression, and give a more broad-minded approach and perspective to their surroundings.

Each sign in a pair seeks and is attracted to the qualities of its complementary opposing sign. Cancer searches for the power and endurance of Capricorn, while Capricorn seeks the softness and understanding of Cancer. Cancer dwells within the realm of the establishment of *personal* security and structure, while Capricorn resides in the realm of the establishment of *social* security and structure.

Although the word 'opposite' conjures up feelings of separateness and differences, the astrological polarities should not be seen as two signs in conflict with each other - their positive expression is to create a natural balance and equilibrium. Each sign has something to learn from its opposite, but also has a contribution to make towards the other sign's more evolved expression. The Fourth (Cancer) and Tenth (Capricorn) House polarity is concerned with the inner world or 'home' versus the outer world or 'vocation'.

Cancer's Fourth House represents inward activity and motivational drives resulting from your home life and upbringing, while the Tenth house is the outward manifestation of them, the bringing of them into the public life. It is with the Fourth House whose cusp indicates the lowest heavens (the I.C.) that we find the foundations of an individual's life. This area represents your environment, background, heritage, where your roots are, and where your personality took shape. Opposite on the axis, is the Tenth House, where an individual must 'earn' her wings; similarly, it could be said that Cancer represents your given, inherited qualities to a large degree, while Capricorn symbolises that which you must work diligently for. The Fourth House contains all the markers you need to grow into yourself, and its opposite is where you must carve out your own mark on the world. It is here, in Capricorn's domain, where you are creating your own markers, to stand out and apart from others as a separate entity in your own right, which is usually expressed through your professional self. Here is where you will acquire your own moral, social, and of course material independence and earn your freedom. But it is also important to remember that to reach this goal with as much serenity and harmony as possible, that you first have strong roots. If your roots are unstable in any way, it can be easy to live through Capricorn's less favourable traits: operating through a superiority complex to mask insecurities, which will force you to rise ever higher, to dominate, rule and conquer both on the social and material front. At the other end, you may never fulfil your ambitions, nor evolve because of a lack of self-confidence, conviction, nerve or courage. How you assert your individuality in the wider world will depend largely on your natural family background and your familial roots. In any case, Capricorn can teach you how to unfold your wings when you are ready to liberate yourself in a worldlier sense, for she is the master of this realm. Through the lessons of the Goat, the Crab can dare to expose herself to the gaze of others, fulfil a mission or role in society, take a firmer stand, flaunt herself, and take up a professional career or post with crystal-clear clarity and purpose.

Career, achievement and what the world remembers you for (Tenth House), are all outer expressions of independence and maturity, but they also have a strong link with the early home environment, security and upbringing (Fourth House). These two houses represent the 'parents' who are psychologically and emotionally important to every individual. Planets in these houses and the signs on the cusps, will indicate the importance of your home and career lives, and the balance between the two.

Negative and Cardinal, this Water-Earth polarity compares the fluctuating femininity of the Moon with the rigid structure of Saturn. It concerns the breadwinner versus the homemaker; the father versus the mother; the unconditional parent versus the conditional parent; the disciplinarian versus the nurturer. Both the Goat and the Crab have the initiating power of Cardinality, but with your negative yin receptivity, both signs are also paradoxical. Cancer knows the emotional value of family, tradition and roots but has a lack of practical ambition. The Cancerian may also be easily influenced, sensitive to others' needs, and may only indirectly achieve her aims. Capricorn demonstrates the attitude needed to succeed in the world and shows how to build something solid and of lasting value, but often this is achieved at the expense of human feeling. Caring, sympathy and kindness can get lost in the discipline and authority of Capricorn's nature, but Capricorn's structure can be softened by Lunar Cancer's influence, and Cancer can teach Capricorn much about feelings and sensitivity.

Capricorn is controlled, closed, emotionally inhibited, self-disciplined, insensitive, stoic, cold, detached, isolated, unresponsive, fathering, sets limits, controlling, exercises power and authority, self-sufficient, industrious, determined, grounded, highly conscious, attuned to external realities, success-oriented, ambitious, seeks public recognition, is concerned with the professional and material, and desires professional security. Cancer relates to emotional fulfilment, the family relations and nurturing the self. It also relates to the looking after of others while ignoring one's own concerns.

Cancer is moody, emotionally unstable, fluid, sensitive, vulnerable, empathetic, sympathetic, responsive, mothering, smothering, nurturing, protective, pampering, attached, dependent, passive, timid, retreating, private, psychic, hidden, intuitive, attuned to the unconscious, develops roots, seeks personal nourishment, is concerned with the personal and domestic, is family or home-oriented, and desires family security.

Capricorn relates to self-responsibility and emotional balance; two traits the Crab definitely needs to incorporate into her character. However, Capricorn also relates to the measuring of success in material terms, and living by the code of one's status. Depending upon how you apply this to yourself, will determine the outcome of your success or otherwise. Capricorn can be mean, which is not something you should take on board yourself; perhaps you could develop an impenetrable status code for yourself that holds you in good stead when you feel you are faltering. The Goat can teach you much about not getting wet in the rain. You are both shrewd, but the Goat gets by on greater wits and cleverness than does the reticent Crab, who prefers to hide while the storm passes.

The Crab also tends to behave like a child for as long as she can get away with it, and has an instinctive need to be needed and protected by others. As well as nurturing others as much as you can, you love a bit of pampering in return. There is something a little bit endearing and enchanting in this, but in the long term it may become grating on those you love.

As a typical Crab, you have spent a large portion of your life investing time and care in others' needs without having proper regard for your own. Although this self-sacrifice and deep devotion to helping others is noble, sometimes a little Capricorn-themed edge can help boost your life. Your own emotional fulfilment is often put on the backburner as you tend to the wants and needs of your closed loved ones, particularly those of your family and children. Capricorn can teach you how to strive a little higher in order to fulfil your own potential; in simple terms, this requires working on your personal ambition and applying it to a wider world than your familial circle. The Goat, in her inherent wisdom, seeks status, power, authority, recognition and worldly goals, and has much to teach you in relation to attaining these for yourself and putting yourself out there on a wider scale.

The powerful self within you may have been crippled in some way by inhibiting conditions or circumstances, particularly those concerning your mother, your childhood or outside threats to your immense need for security. As a result, you often quite literally clam up and seek refuge in your shell. You have had plenty of practice in the art of loving kindness and softness, but Capricorn can help you develop a tougher outer shell which not only protects you, but allows for onward and upward movement into your higher self.

The sensitive, fluid, responsible, instinctive, feeling-oriented individual, easily influenced by others and living through them (Cancer) seeks the structure, self-motivation and self-reliance which is the fruit of individual effort (Capricorn). The disciplined and self-motivated individual, capable of mastering the environment through the harnessing of self-propelled energy (Capricorn) seeks the warmth and security of human relationships, the embrace of close others and intimate feeling exchange (Cancer).

The Goat will tell you to stop being sentimental, blot your tears and move on from that sort of behaviour. You yearn for tenderness and comfort since you allow yourself to be guided by your anxious nature and because you are never quite able to live or act alone. Your complementary opposite Capricorn can help you by encouraging an increased self-confidence to branch out on your own and embrace greater self-control to enable you to acquire social, emotional, relational and professional independence. Capricorn is a master of autonomy in all facets of life, and can teach Cancer the tools of the trade.

It is not surprising that Cancer may feel slightly put off or intimidated by the Capricorn's smooth, astute manner of self-promotion. With sensitive

Moon-ruled Cancer, the sign of nurturing and the past, and no-nonsense Saturn-ruled Capricorn, the sign of judgement and ascension, you may feel daunted by your opposite's lessons; after all, she is a bossy, stern and often mean-spirited, teacher. But clinging to your old and tested methods of self-comfort will not shield you from the fact that Capricorn's lessons, although harsh, are simply reality checks that can only serve to propel you further along your astral journey. Like your fellow Water sign Pisces, you are prone to burying your head in the sand when confronted with duty or responsibility, but this will only deepen your suffering and hinder your progress. You may wish for someone to supply answers, protect you, pick up the pieces or hear your distress and make it all better - and Capricorn can indeed be there to provide these, but only to a certain extent. Capricorn does not take prisoners, and is forever pressing onward. She has no time for self-pity and will tell you to pick yourself up, dust yourself off and keep climbing skyward. You need to hear this call to duty as it will benefit you. But what's more, you have to do it for *yourself*. Capricorn can teach you a greater sense of independence which you so desperately need to learn if you wish to move on from the bondage of your past.

Indeed, the Goat teaches you to release your pampered or protected past. No more getting lost in confusion or chaos, she tells you. You need not to fear change or the abandonment of your comfort zone, for paradoxically, you can only attain true security once you let go of all those fears and dependencies. Cancer's characteristic profound sensitivity and vulnerability can be transformed into deep ambition and achievements, when you decide to listen to this message.

In essence, the Goat is here to force the Crab to grow up. Cancer needs to realise that she can't hide behind her mummy or daddy, play in the perennial sandbox or swan around the safe shallows forever. You need to swallow your fears, release your insecurities and trust the Capricorn when she holds your hand and leads you into the wider adult Universe. For the Goat knows perhaps better than anyone, that there is a whole world of accomplishment waiting for you out there. So take a bold leap of faith out of your comfort zone!

WHAT THE GOAT CAN ULTIMATELY TEACH THE CRAB

Release ★ Subjectivity, the need to be protected, being overprotective, irrational fears, sulkiness, fear of others, clinginess, possessiveness, dwelling in the past, soppiness, defeatist attitudes, negative habits, using others as a crutch, co-dependence, smothering your family, deep-rooted insecurities

Embrace ★ Objectivity, ownership of feelings, trust, striving toward the future, social independence, personal ambition, career success, self-control, self-discipline, responsibility, a sense of duty, self-assurance, inner strength, perseverance

"If you love something, set it free; if it never comes back it was never meant to be."

The Goat can teach the Crab about nurturing the self as well as others; to love without smothering; to develop objectivity; to liberate yourself from familial obligations from time to time; to know that security is yours if you learn to trust and let go; to stop clinging to the past; to climb a little higher than you feel comfortable with; to leave the bounds of your comfort zone; to be more ambitious and direct; to let down your guard and express your feelings outwardly and with greater authority; to own your feelings; to practice greater self-control and autonomy to enable you to acquire greater all-round independence and success.

There is a wonderful hermetic and alchemical 'law' which is the concept "as within, so without" - in all her self-assuredness and sure-footedness, the Capricorn instinctually knows that her inner strength will fuel her onward trip, and carries on her journey with little fear, apprehension or worry about what the top of the mountain will actually look like - for her only concern lies in getting there in the first place. And she has only achieved this feat in attitude by leaving the restrictions of her comfort zones and leaving behind the roots that bind, to enable her to climb higher than she ever dreamed possible. And as Capricornian Martin Luther King so wisely put: "You don't have to see the whole staircase. Just take the first step."

MAGIC, DRAWING, ATTRACTION, SPELLS, RITUALS, WISHING & POWER

A Note on the Universe

Within each of us resides the merging of the Sun and the Moon, the dance of the constellations, the vibrations of the planets, and the vast microcosm and macrocosm of the entire *Universe*. Uni means 'one' and Verse means 'song'; therefore, the word Universe literally means 'One Song'. If you learn to tune yourself in, you can even hear it!

What is Magic?

Magic is a kind of special energy that is beyond description, and like most kinds of energy it has its own rules and ways of being manipulated. It remains an elusive term, and no definition has ever really found Universal acceptance. Attempts to separate it from superstition, religion and other-worldly phenomena on the one hand, and 'science' on the other, are ridden with difficulties. However slippery the term 'magic' might be, there is a general agreement that most of us wish for more of its presence in our lives and often fall short of achieving this wish.

Those performing spells, 'asking the Universe', wishing, praying, or undertaking rituals, are using this very special energy to draw things to them. Learning to manipulate energy in these ways is never hard (and shouldn't be), but it can be complex and does require knowledge, practice, creativity, patience and above all, imagination. Most of us use simple magic every day, whether by saying little prayers, making wishes, visualising, and exchanging - sending out and receiving - good, positive or hopeful vibes. When you understand that all the forces and magic you need are *within* you, and you learn to *believe* in that power, you are then able to make all manner of changes to your life and, most importantly, yourself.

Magic is an invisible force which connects and permeates everything. Every thought you have and every action you take, will affect the strength of this force, and can be influenced and directed towards a specific purpose by using certain means. The most important of these are your intentions, facing in the direction of your desired outcome, your will and your *belief* that it works. The more you want something to happen, and the clearer you can visualise the desired outcome, the stronger your will and feelings towards it will be, ensuring an avalanche of amazing people, events and circumstances will flow into your experiences, gathering speed, momentum and power as it nears your goal or dream.

The Universe (or whichever higher power you believe in) works for us and through us. Ideas are given to us but they must be carried out *through* us, in the form of asking or acting or performing a ritual or casting a specific spell. The Universe's abundance is your abundance, and it flows through your mind into manifestation. The Universe or Divine Being in which you believe, gives you the necessary ideas and clothes them with all that is needed to bring them into form when we ask *believing*.

Based on ancient human beliefs, systems and superstitions, declaring what you want and acting out your deepest desires can actually help to make things happen. Magical ideas include the notion that thought affects matter and that the trained imagination can alter the physical world, that all aspects of the Universe are interdependent and that we can discover connections and correspondences between everyday occurrences and cosmic, or Divine, energies. A miracle or a wish coming true can suggest something is going on that extends beyond the laws of nature, that something unseen has occurred; but just because we cannot see it or touch it, it doesn't mean it's not there. Magic exists, especially if you truly believe it does, but science is so far incapable of capturing its essence or the rationale behind it. Personally, I prefer to leave that task to the higher powers of the Universe.

To help your dreams come true and to use your inborn power to its full effect, you can employ boosters based on the special energies and qualities of your Sun sign. These 'boosters' are chosen to be in alignment with the purpose of a particular goal, and contain energies of their own which will enhance the strength of your spell, prayer, ritual or 'asking'. Specific magical energies can be invoked by carrying out a spell or ceremony using specific herbs or colours, or on a particular day of the week, according to either your Sun sign (to heighten the power of the asking), and/or that is in sympathy with that for which you are asking (I have included days of the week for other Sun signs and spell types).

Some materials and boosters you can use to increase the power, magic or energy in any area of your life include: candles, wish lists (written on an appropriate piece of paper written with a specially-chosen writing tool), symbols, affirmations, chants, incense, herbs and flowers, locations, colours, days of the week, elements, crystals and gemstones, animal symbols, charms, talismans, amulets, gods and goddesses, essential oils, planetary hours and your Solar totem animals. All are covered, some more briefly than others, for your very special Sun sign to radiate the energy to powerfully draw your wildest dreams towards you!

Overall, it pays to remember that the Universe (or whatever higher power/s or force/s you happen to believe in) creates *through* you that to which you give your attention. What you contemplate becomes the law of your being, and through your pure unwavering belief, is eventually brought through to manifestation on the material plane. What you think about is entirely up to you. But just be mindful that whatever you think about the most becomes your dominant thought, then your main point of attraction, and is ultimately magnified until it becomes your reality or your experience. So choose your thoughts with care. And to quote Ralph Waldo Emerson, "Be careful what you set your heart upon, for it will surely be yours." I carry a copy of this beautiful prophecy in my purse as its words resonate so strongly with me. In other words, be mindful about what you're wishing for, for you will most probably get it, whether it's good or bad - magic, after all, doesn't discriminate. Just make your dominant thoughts good ones, and you will attract everything you set your heart and intentions upon. Good luck!

ASTROLOGY & MAGIC

"Everyone practices magic, whether they realise it or not, for magic is the art of attracting particular influences, events and situations within human life. Magic is a natural phenomenon because the Universe is reflexive, responding to human thoughts, aspirations and desires ..."
David Fideler, *Jesus Christ, Sun of God*

Astrology is the most sublime of the occult * sciences, while at the same time it is one of the most practical for everyday application, for it divines the human soul itself. The cosmos, particularly the patterns that formed across it at the exact moment we were born, indicates the road along which our mental and spiritual endowments are likely to impel us, therefore enabling us to prepare in advance for life's battles, pitfalls, milestones, celebrations and of course to make the utmost of opportunities. Such is the magic of the human mind, that it can 'see' into the future and relive the past without having to be physically present in either, and when combined with astrological *knowing*, particularly the knowing that springs from understanding some of the dynamics of our natal chart, however basic, our inner - and outer - magic can be lifted to phenomenal heights.

In ancient times, not only was astrology the ardent study of the most learned and powerful minds, but among the masses of ordinary people its authority and guidance was accepted and followed without question. How this powerful knowledge was used was - and still is - up to the individual, but all who used it applied it to their perceived advantage.

As primitive humans observed the skies, no doubt they gradually realised that certain stars upon which their fate depended accompanied the seasons, or certain times of the year. They may also have reasoned that if governed their fate, they also governed their bodies, and it is therefore conceivable that the skies were associated with Divine influence. Certain celestial influences were believed to emanate from the thirty-six decans of the signs, and the mysterious but apparent effect that they exercised upon humans were thought to be due to a subtle ether shed by the heavenly stars and spheres on the Earth, that affected not only people, but also other animals, plants and minerals. For the ancient mind, linking magic with astrology may have also provided a much needed sense of predictability and patterns.

Early astrologers named and made associations with the imaginary divisions of the twelve signs and the twelve houses, and people born under a certain sign were said to inherit to an extent, its properties and nature. They also believed that the influence of the planets and stars corresponded with the medicinal properties of certain plants and minerals. They therefore asserted that the influence of a star or planetary position would affect the type of medicine or healing they would offer a subject to attain the most beneficial outcome. Throughout the writings of early philosophers and theorists, there is constant reference to this unmistakable mystic connection between the seven known planets and Earthly affairs and ailments. The seven metals were connected with the seven planets, to which the seven colours and the seven transformations were added. So the alchemist came to share the astrological doctrine that each planet ruled some mineral: the Sun ruled gold, the Moon silver, Mars iron, Venus copper, Saturn lead, Jupiter tin, and Mercury quicksilver. Consequently, in alchemical symbolism the same sign came to represent the metal and its corresponding planet.

In subsequent years, astrology became closely related to alchemical knowledge and development, and the alchemist came to be regarded as an authority not only on the transmutation of metals, but also on astrology and magic. This goes some of the way to explaining how magic and divination, which had always been inseparably bound up with astrology, came to be associated with alchemy. In all the occult sciences, the supreme power was believed to be in the stars above, and from their mysterious emanations all the metals, crystals, minerals, plants and herbs derived their special properties over time. Further, as alchemy became ever more spiritual and concerned with more abstract and philosophical concepts, eventually it was considered that the transmutation of lead into gold was simply a metaphor for the transformation of base matter, in this case the human soul, into a much purer and higher state of wisdom and being.

The Sun and Moon were believed to have greater influence over the human body than all the other heavenly bodies, and to exert their influence in various ways whenever they entered a certain sign of the zodiac. And although the Moon was traditionally regarded as the most important factor of a horoscope, the Sun has come into its own in later centuries, with the result that almost everyone knows their Sun sign but only those who have delved deeper are aware of the sign their natal Moon falls in. For this reason, I have chosen to focus this book series on the twelve Sun signs, as this is what the majority of people are most familiar with.

The following pages contain methods, energies, materials and objects which may be used to increase the magic and power of your Sun sign's influence upon you. Precious stones, flowers, colours and so on, are regarded as having a potent effect upon good fortune by attuning your mind to receive harmonious vibrations from the astral forces that surround you.

Finally, a basic working knowledge of basic astronomy and astrology is an asset when working with luck, abundance, wealth and personal power. You can attract more of these things when you align yourself with the workings of the wider Universe, the movement of the Sun, stars, Moon and planets and become aware of the correlations between the outer cycles of the skies and the inner cycles within yourself. Also, for those who are knowledgeable about Moon phases, equinoxes and solstices, a world of lucky possibilities can also magically open up to you. You don't need to know about astrology's deepest complexities to understand how everything interrelates; just learning the basics will give you an edge - and hopefully the following lucky tips will provide you with at least a small glimpse into the insights gleaned from your Sun sign, which I am certain will endow upon you the potential for amazing results to manifest in your life - and maybe even a step up one further rung towards the heavens!

* The word 'occult' comes from the Latin *occultus*, which literally means 'knowledge of the hidden'.

USING COLOURS, CRYSTALS, DEITIES, PLANTS, FOODS & MATERIAL SUBSTANCES FOR INCREASING POWER & MAGNETISING MAGIC

Alchemist, reformer and mystic Henry Cornelius Agrippa, born in 1486, in his principal work, *On Occult Philosophy*, expressed his belief in the doctrines of astrology and in the theory that the spirit of the world exists in the body of the world, just as the human spirit exists in the body of man. He contended that this spirit also abounds in the celestial bodies and descends in the rays of stars, so that the things influenced by their rays become conformable to them. By this spirit every occult property is conveyed into metals, stones, herbs and animals, through the Sun, Moon and planets, and even through the stars beyond and higher than the planets. A firm believer in the efficacy of charms, he stated that they may "be worn on the body bound to any part of it or hung around the neck, changing sickness into health or health into sickness." I believe the same effect could be applied to wishing and the thinking of positive thoughts, to mean, "Changing thoughts and dreams into manifest reality." He also recommended that these charms be worn in the form of finger rings (that have been created using the materials in agreement and harmony with your Sun Sign's magical energy).

Material substances are connected with abstract purposes by a complex but highly usable and accessible system of correspondences. Use these time-honoured connections in your own spells and wishes to magnetise your desires to you. The following pages will give you some materials, energies, forces and ideas you can summon the power of in order to enhance your magic and luck.

PLANETS

The planetary influence of the day is important when 'asking' for something. If you are wishing for luck, for example, try working with your Sun sign's inherent energies combined with the perfect day of the week for it. So a Cancerian might try using her natural intuitive powers and intellect, to ask for greater luck on a Thursday, which is Jupiter's Day and Jupiter is renowned for being a lucky planet, or better still, ask for luck on a Monday, which is the Moon's Day, ruler of Cancer, at the time of day when Jupiter's influence is at its most powerful (information about planetary hours for each day of the week can be found on the Internet or in books on the subject, and can be complex and detailed. It is an art to memorise the correct times, days and energies for the correct spells. If you are determined enough to achieve your dream or goal however, you will be determined enough to put in the research to do it properly!) Here is a very simplified list of the days of the week and their meanings:

DAYS OF THE WEEK & THEIR POWERS

MONDAY ★ Moon
Cancer

The Divine feminine, changes, intuition, emotions, secrets, dealing with women, purity, goodness, perfection, unity, psychic ability, magic, spirituality, invoking a goddess's or angel's guidance, anything that fluctuates, contracts, increases or decreases.

TUESDAY ★ Mars
Aries & Scorpio

Enthusiasm, competition, passion, energy, courage, protection, victory, anything requiring assertiveness, standing up for yourself, or a 'fighting spirit', determination, vitality, sexuality, self-confidence, men's power, men's mysteries, drive, ambition, achievement, triumph, masculinity.

WEDNESDAY ★ Mercury
Gemini & Virgo

Education, travel, exams, study, communication, making connections, thinking, dealing with siblings, writing and speaking, knowledge, learning, adaptability, charm, youth, absorbing information.

THURSDAY ★ Jupiter
Sagittarius & Pisces

Increase and expansion of anything (remember to be careful what you wish for), luck, growth, influence, worldly power, accomplishment, fulfilment, gambling, philosophy, higher education, abundance, optimism.

FRIDAY ★ Venus
Taurus & Libra

Love, luxury, the arts, indulgence, beauty, marriage, money, prosperity, fertility, women's power, women's mysteries, grace, charm, appeal, hope, pleasure, decorating, self-worth, self-esteem, personal values, business partnerships, romance, creativity, sharing, bonding.

SATURDAY ★ Saturn
Capricorn & Aquarius

Long-term goals, career, institutions, establishments, security, investments, karma, reversal, structure, protection, solitude, privacy, determination, ending, blocking, renewing, transforming, anything to do with the public.

SUNDAY ★ Sun
Leo

All-purpose, success, wishes, generosity, happiness, optimism, spirit/essence, recognition, health, vitality, material wealth, invoking a god's aid or guidance, personal empowerment, spirituality, the Divine masculine.

YOUR NATAL MOON PHASE

Although this book is aimed at enhancing your life through the energy of your Sun sign, a bit of Lunar help can give your wishing a boost! As well as using the planetary days and hours system to add a bit of zest to your wish fulfilment, try combining your Sun sign's power periods with your natal Moon phase (your natal Moon phase can be calculated using a number of sources on the internet, or through an astrologer), or even studying which constellation the Moon is situated in at certain times, to increase the power of your spells and asking rituals. For example, you might like to 'ask' for a promotion at work during a New/Waxing Moon period, particularly if the Moon happens to fall under an auspicious sign for career advancement, such as Capricorn. Your natal Moon phase can also be used to similar effect, by researching when your Moon phase will coincide with a certain Lunar constellation position.

In most astrological interpretations the Sun is regarded as the most important, central feature of a natal chart. But to many the Moon is equally, if not more, important than the Sun sign. Many ancient cultures considered the Moon sign to be more significant. The Moon passes through the 12 signs about every 2.5 days, usually covering the whole zodiac in around 27.3 days. The Moon symbolises our inner world, the world of feeling, emotions, habitual responses, instincts, intuition, security and the subconscious. It describes our nurturing style and needs, our emotional response to life, our attitudes and likely reactions to others, our instinctive and habitual responses, the receptive feminine side of ourselves, our experience of our mother or mother figure, and our childhood experience. It represents the soul. In relationships it symbolises how we like to be nurtured and cared for, and the potential depth of our involvement on personal intimate levels.

For many centuries, people across the world have recognised that the Moon influences the affairs of all living things on planet Earth. The waxing Moon appears to have a drawing, increasing and enhancing effect, whereas the waning Moon has a decreasing, receding and withdrawing effect. All things that come into being are stamped with the qualities of the prevailing Moon stage. It seems that people born during certain Lunar phases tend to share specific attributes with other people born during this same phase. In turn, their attributes will be subtly different from those of individuals born during any of the other stages in the Moon cycle. Knowing exactly which phase of the Moon you were born under gives you all kinds of extraordinarily valuable insights into your character, emotions, behaviour and motivations in life. It can make you aware of your deepest underlying drives, the fundamental purpose that you are drawn towards in life and the contribution you can make to others and society during the course of your lifetime. This knowledge may enable you to intuit and make the most of your own personal cyclical pattern that you go through each month, and allow you to know when the most auspicious periods of time are for you and your affairs, nurture yourself and channel your energies in the most positive directions.

Because this Lunar pattern repeats itself every month, you will find that you can even pace yourself on a long-term basis. This will enable you to effectively target your efforts and goals on periods of time that you know will be potentially fortunate for you. You may in fact find that your birth phase corresponds with the days of the month when you have abundant energy, feel inspired and can generate new ideas with ease. During this period, you should work towards the fruition of your efforts, bring your dreams into light and reach for the stars!

The Lunar Phases Are:
★ New Moon
★ First/Waxing Crescent
★ First Quarter
★ Waxing Gibbous Moon
★ Full Moon
★ Waning Gibbous / Disseminating Moon
★ Last Quarter
★ Waning Crescent / Balsamic Moon
★ Back to the New Moon

SPELLS, MAGIC & WISHING WITH MOON PHASES

Though the Moon has eight astronomical phases, it is the three phases corresponding to maiden, mother and crone that are the most significant in spells, ritual, wish magic and psychic work. By tuning into the physical Moon we can understand and harness these distinct energy phases in our daily lives and magical worlds. The four primary Lunar phases are the New Moon, First Quarter, Full Moon and the Last Quarter. Depending on what sort of spell you wish to perform, your spell should take place during one of these cycles or time periods. Each phase of the Moon is good for some types of magic, but not so much for others.

NEW MOON, WAXING & FIRST QUARTER

In astronomical terms, the New Moon occurs when the Moon rises and sets at the same time as the Sun. Both bodies are found in the same position compared with the Earth. Therefore, a Solar eclipse can only ever occur at the New Moon, when the two luminaries are found, for a short time, in a perfect line relative to the Earth, with the Moon positioned between the Sun and the Earth. The New Moon's sunlit face is hidden from the Earth.

In astrological terms, the New Moon occurs at a time when the Sun and the Moon are found in the same degree of the zodiac and therefore occupy the same zodiac sign, forming a conjunction, or a 'fusing' of energies.

In astronomical terms, the First Quarter occurs seven days after the New Moon. Seen from the Earth, this phase makes the Moon like a crescent, forming the shape of a capital D.

In astrological terms, it occurs when the Sun and the Moon form a ninety-degree angle, or the square aspect, inside the zodiac, the Moon always preceding the Sun.

As the New Moon marks the beginning of a new cycle, it symbolises fresh starts. This is an exceptional time to work magic and make wishes for new beginnings, and for the conception and initiation of new projects. Use this Moon phase for improving health, the gradual increase of prosperity, attracting good luck, fertility magic, finding new love, friendship or romance, job hunting, making plans for the future and increasing your general spiritual or psychic awareness.

Overall, the Waxing Crescent and First Quarter Moon phases are appropriate for spells, rituals and workings that involve growth, healing and increase. This is a period of time lasting approximately two weeks, to draw things toward you and increase things, such as love, prosperity and new opportunities. During this period is the time to bless new projects, anything that requires energy to grow, such as gardens, business ventures, new homes, or educational pursuits. Personal growth and healing are accented, as is 'attraction magic' - drawing something to you such as love, abundance, health, success or a new path - and if done well, you can expect results by the next Full Moon. Magical workings for gain, increase or bringing things to you should be initiated when the Moon is waxing (or New, going from Dark to Full). A time for divination of all kinds, spells of spiritual intention, and for any creative project you wish to see birthed, with magical and fruitful results.

While making a wish within the first forty-eight hours after the New Moon is a powerful way of helping it come to fruition, the most potent time for making wishes is actually within the first eight hours of the exact time of its position. Write down your wish list within this first eight hours on a piece of appropriately coloured paper with a special writing tool, and be sure to capture the essence of your wish by wording it in a way that charges your emotions and simply feels 'right'. Make a maximum of ten wishes (less is perfectly fine too), as making too many wishes might disperse their energy too much to be effective. After writing down your list and releasing your wishes to the Universe in whichever form you feel happy with, keep your list and check on it in a few days', weeks' or months' time to assess whether anything has shifted in the direction of your listed dreams, desires or goals. I'll bet it has - or at the very least, something even better has arrived in its place!

Although the first forty-eight hours after the New Moon is the most potent time to make a special wish, you can begin Waxing Moon magic when you can see the crescent in the sky and continue until the day before the Full Moon. The closer to the Full Moon, the more intense the energies. In fact, a personally devised ritual using any special Lunar-associated materials over three days up to and including the Full Moon is excellent for something you require urgently or within a short timeframe.

In some cultures, people turn over silver coins or jewellery three times when the crescent Moon appears in the sky and make a wish. As the Moon grows, it is believed that prosperity and good fortune will grow too.

While the New Moon is not known as a time for 'banishing' or releasing things we no longer want in our lives, I feel that if we are to ask and wish for things, we need to make room to receive them. Making room means that the Universe can slot it right into our lives where we have cleared our paths for it. Clutter, unwanted things, unhappy relationships, possessions that no longer serve us, are all things we can banish. So, to help what you are asking for come into your life quicker, the New Moon is a particularly opportune time to throw a few things out so you can make way for the new and clear up some space for that which you are wishing for. What are you waiting for? Start creating a space for your wishes today!

FULL MOON

In astronomical terms, the Full Moon occurs 14 days after the New Moon, on the day when the Moon sets at the same time the Sun rises, or conversely. The two luminaries are effectively facing each other, with the Earth in between, the Sun shining its light onto the reflective Moon, giving it the fully lit up appearance of a giant, bright, perfectly round sphere. Indeed, its entire face is bathed in sunlight. A Lunar eclipse can only occur at the Full Moon, when the Sun, Moon and Earth are all in line, and the Earth hides the lit side of the Moon to us.

In astrological terms, a Full Moon occurs at the time when the Sun and Moon are 180 degrees apart inside the zodiac, and therefore positioned in opposite signs, forming an opposition aspect.

The highest energy occurs at the Full Moon, making this is a powerful time for all manner of magical workings. Use the Full Moon phase for any immediate need, a sudden boost of power or courage, psychic protection, a change of career or location, travel, healing acute health conditions, the consummation of love or a commitment, justice, ambition and promotion of all kinds. This phase lasts approximately 3 days - 24 hours before the exact Full Moon, the day of, and 24 hours after it, according to many sources - giving us 3 full days to perform our spells. However, we are not strictly limited to a three-day period; the power of this phase can actually be accessed for seven days - three days prior to, the night of, and the three days after the Full Moon. The Full Moon period is when the Moon is at her most powerful, being the most luminous and radiant part of the cycle. Known as the 'high tide' of psychic power, the Full Moon represents culmination, climax, fulfilment and abundance. The Full Moon governs all kinds of magic, including manifestation, banishing, and is particularly good for calling forth protection and heightening your intuitive abilities. The Full Moon contains magic that calls forth personal power, fertility, spiritual development, and psychic awareness. Cleansing of ritual tools, crystals, wish lists, Tarot decks, and the like can be done during this phase. Magic worked during the Full Moon often takes one complete cycle to come to fruition. Try also reaffirming your desires during the New Moon to give them an added nudge in the right direction.

LAST QUARTER OR WANING MOON

In astronomical terms, the Last Quarter, or Waning Moon, occurs twenty-one days after the New Moon. The time difference between the rising and setting of the two luminaries is reduced to what it was at the First Quarter. Viewed from the Earth, the Moon resembles a crescent whose lit up area is decreasing in size, forming the shape of a capital C.

In astrological terms, the Waning Moon occurs when the Sun and Moon are positioned at ninety degree angles of each other in the zodiac, forming the square aspect again. However, during this phase, the Sun is instead *ahead* of the Moon.

The Waning Moon represents the Lunar cycle from Full to Dark. Any spells and magic performed during this period is based purely around banishing and releasing. It could involve releasing things which no longer serve you (such as behaviours, material things, relationships and attitudes), banishing negative energies, and removing obstacles which are standing in the way of achieving your goals or dreams. The Waning Moon is the best time for cleansing, gently releasing, eliminating, expelling and completion. It is of great assistance when you are wanting to let go of something, or someone, gradually. The Dark of the Moon, the period when the Moon is no longer visible to the naked eye, until the New Moon, is the most useful time for divination of all kinds.

★ What is your natal Moon phase type?
Can you think of ways you can combine it with the power of your Sun sign to effect change and bring about wonderful happenings? ★

HARNESSING YOUR PERSONAL MOON MAGIC ★ MOON IN CANCER

When the Moon is in your sign of Cancer, it is in its natural home, where it is most comfortable and harmonious. Therefore, it is a great time for working magic around: Moon worship and wishing, females in general, emotions, psychism, intuition, bringing your dreams out of the night and into the light of day, peace, domestic bliss, protection, magnetism, sympathy, and all things maternal or to do with the Mother. Suggested operations could be around rituals and spells involving female friendships and relationships (and if you are a female, your relationship with yourself), the feminine Divine, calling forth the powers of female goddesses, protection of yourself or loved ones, increasing your psychic awareness, transforming unhelpful emotions into positive ones, dreams, divination of all kinds, and telepathy. It is also an opportune time to tap into your feminine side (even if you are a male) by incorporating yin symbols into your environment. With the Moon in Cancer, domestic harmony is accentuated and the relationship with one's mother, mother figure or strongest feminine role model is also emphasised, so this period is great for working with these energies.

THE MOON ★
WHAT IT REPRESENTS
IN THE HUMAN PSYCHE &
NATAL CHART

The Moon in the sky shines with the reflected light of the Sun. Although not a planet, the Moon is our nearest celestial neighbour and exerts a great influence upon us. The gravitational pull of the Moon affects our body fluids, which contribute to about 90 per cent of our biological make-up. It moves at approximately half a degree per hour and takes an average of 27.3 days to pass through all twelve zodiac signs, staying in each for around 2.5 days.

In astrology the Moon corresponds with the way in which we reflect and respond to what is going on around us. It has to do with our feelings, emotions and instincts and, in the same way the Moon influences the tides on planet Earth, it symbolises the ebb and flow of our emotional nature, our moods, fluctuations and changeability. The Moon is the archetype of the Mother, which is within us all, and represents the primary feminine principle in the natal chart. It is through the Moon that we express our parental instincts - caring, nurturing, protecting, and sensitivity. The Moon has links with the past and the subconscious and it is from this almost primitive source that our natural instinctual forces flow.

The Moon is essentially a feminine principle and associates with the inner personality, receptivity, passivity and inward-oriented feelings. It can act as an inner guide to the deeper self, the unconscious self, figures half-shrouded in mystery, linking the hidden personal world of the subconscious to the clearer world of personal awareness.

The Moon is the innermost core of our being, private feelings, habitual reactions and subconscious habits. It is the caring, nurturing sustainer of life, the 'mother' of the zodiac. It tells us about how we seek security, our urge to nurture, our nurturing style, our responses and feelings and moods. The innermost core of our being, private feelings, subconscious habits. It is concerned with habits, mothering, habitual/instinctive responses and personality. It is our karma, our soul, our past.

The Moon represents our mother or mother figure, our feminine side, maternal instinct, our nurturing style and needs, our unconscious self, our emotional reactions, the subconscious, our feelings, instincts, intuition, receptivity, habits, what we need to feel secure, fluctuations, cycles, moods, and our childhood. Its position in the birth chart is very significant, because as well as revealing feminine qualities and the potential gentleness and tenderness of a being, the Moon also reveals important information about the experiences and expression of the five senses.

The Moon is essentially receptive and passive; it reflects the life experience rather than initiating it. Fluctuating and cyclical, the Moon is the planet (although technically a satellite) of the childhood experience, and instinctual reactions. It represents the mother (a child's experience and expectations of their mother), maternal instincts and the feminine principle, indicating how strongly these manifest in an individual, male or female.

As it represents what our childhood experience is likely to be, and childhood is essentially a time where our consciousness has not yet fully developed, our Moon sign traits seem to be more apparent in our younger years. We will usually show our Moon sign traits more so than our Sun sign traits during this developing period of infancy and early childhood, until we have the presence of mind to more consciously develop our ego and true core self (the Sun).

The symbol for the Moon ☾ is a representation of its crescent in its waxing phase from new to full, but it can also be seen as two half circles - these form a bowl shape, a receptacle, a feminine container that 'receives' and 'holds' anything put into it. The half circle, unlike the full circle of the Sun, is finite and incomplete, almost as if striving for wholeness.

The Moon represents our *soul*.

YOUR MOON SIGN

The Sun / Moon Polarity
Conscious & Unconscious,
Night & Day, Yin & Yang

"Man does, woman is."
Edward Edinger

Your Moon Sign, representing your soul, and your Sun sign, representing your spirit, work together to form the foundation of your basic personality, expression and nature. If you know what your Moon sign is, look it up below and read how it works with your Cancerian Sun to blend your mind, soul and spirit.

♈ **With the Moon in ARIES,** Sun in Cancer, you are likely to be ★ Sociable, devoted, moody, loyal, sensitive, restless, emotionally expressive, enthusiastic, loyal, temperamental, hot-tempered, sulky, childish, sensitive, ego-based, emotionally bold, a tenacious warrior, shrewd, strong, insightful, vulnerable but brave, active imagination, loving, protective, demonstrative, affectionate, creative, gentle but spirited, dependent yet independent, defensive but forthright, receptive, self-assertive, and torn between security and risk.

Sun/Moon Harmony Rating ★ 6 out of 10

♉ **With the Moon in TAURUS,** Sun in Cancer, you are likely to be ★ Gentle, easygoing but moody, pragmatically emotional, traditional, possessive, a homebody, clingy, stubborn, materialistic, security-seeking, patient, loving of home comforts, slow, steady-paced, afraid of change, supportive, comfort-seeking, tenacious, determined, emotionally placid, clannish, domestic, devoted, logical but intuitive, mothering and smothering, imaginative yet grounded, faithful, soft-hearted, tender, resourceful, dependable, modest, peace-loving, considerate, thoughtful, sensible, persistent, and dedicated to your family.

Sun/Moon Harmony Rating ★ *7.5 out of 10*

♊ **With the Moon in GEMINI**, Sun in Cancer, you are likely to be ★ Changeable, friendly, sharing, hospitable, emotionally versatile, self-reflective, a sympathetic conversationalist, whimsically charming, quick-witted and poetically adept, emotionally perceptive and expressive, clever, able to listen to others' needs, quietly sociable, emotionally intelligent, scatterbrained, socially nervous and timid, moody, restless, creative, in possession of a good memory for personal detail, giving, supportive, helpful, understanding, accommodating, responsive, shrewdly perceptive, aware of others' needs, and an effervescent and welcoming host or hostess.

Sun/Moon Harmony Rating ★ *9 out of 10*

♋ **With the Moon in CANCER,** Sun in Cancer, you are likely to be ★ Retentive, passive, sensitive, intuitive, emotional, compassionate, kind, tender, sympathetic, security-seeking, mothering, shy, reticent, hidden, private, eccentric, peaceful, imaginative, poetic, devoted helpful, companionable, self-protective, romantic, secretive, clannish, instinctive, habitual, defensive, home-loving, artistic, attached to the past, nourishing, moody, affectionate, nurturing, tenacious, psychic, easily hurt, evasive, elusive, a worrier, sulky, dependent, and attached to people and possessions.

Sun/Moon Harmony Rating ★ 7 out of 10

♌ **With the Moon in LEO,** Sun in Cancer, you are likely to be ★ Individualistic, aristocratic, shrewd, gentle on the surface with a great strength within, friendly, subtly dramatic, artistic, dramatic, generous in helping others, inspirational, quietly passionate, radiantly loving, affectionate, adoring, caring, romantically imaginative, proud of family, warmly hospitable, charismatic, gently charming, bold, dependent on others, approval-seeking, glamorising of others and failing to see their true colours, modestly ambitious, creative, emotionally radiating warmth, big-hearted, hearty, comfort-loving, loving of creature comforts, helpful, demonstrative, and creatively imaginative. Richard D. Bach's, "It was morning, and the new Sun sparkled gold across the ripples of a gentle sea," perhaps best sums you up.

Sun/Moon Harmony Rating ★ 8 out of 10

♍ **With the Moon in VIRGO,** Sun in Cancer, you are likely to be ★ Imaginatively analysing, dutiful, reflective, attentive, caring, helpful, concerned, sympathetic, loyal, timid, shrewd, fussy, intelligent, solemn, calm and collected, clever, discriminating, an emotional perfectionist, a devoted researcher, serious, kind-hearted, efficient, reserved, emotional yet rational, doubtful, balanced between the feelings and the intellect, altruistic, devoted to others, a good domestic organiser, retiring, introverted, self-controlled, self-contained, introverted, sympathetic but practical, self-doubting, pure, conscientious, prude, private, socially adaptable, able to combine imagination with efficiency, articulate, morally proper, and able to combine compassion and common sense.

Sun/Moon Harmony Rating ★ *7.5 out of 10*

♎ **With the Moon in LIBRA,** Sun in Cancer, you are likely to be ★ Intelligent, sociable, refined, adaptable, generally well-balanced and moderate, easygoing, gentle, affectionate, nervous, people-pleasing, loving, clingy, dependent, graceful, subtly charming, sharing, gracious, cooperative, hospitable, romantically idealistic, endearing, delightful, polite, artistically sensitive, elegant, socially aware, tentative yet eager for attention, sensitive, tender, defensive yet devoted, articulate, peace-loving, concerned for the welfare of others, and dependent on family and close relationships for emotional nourishment.

Sun/Moon Harmony Rating ★ *8 out of 10*

♏ **With the Moon in SCORPIO,** Sun in Cancer, you are likely to be ★ Magnetic, compelling, intensely emotional, formidable, dramatic, defensive, suspicious, powerfully protective of self and others, subtle yet forceful, possessive, vindictive, moody, insightful, probing, committed, strong-willed, initiating, daring, single-minded, cautious, transformative, intensely dedicated, resilient, strong, passionate, unyielding, resourceful, tenacious, investigative, controlling, persevering, tenacious, devoted to loved ones, penetrative, secretive, hidden, unwaveringly loyal, mysterious, unshakable, courageous, exacting, manipulative, intriguing, acutely perceptive, emotionally powerful, and in possession of deep healing capabilities.

Sun/Moon Harmony Rating ★ *7.5 out of 10* **

♐ **With the Moon in SAGITTARIUS,** Sun in Cancer, you are likely to be ★ Warmly loving, colourful, restless, eager, cautious yet adventurous, friendly, idealistic, torn between freedom and security, big-hearted, honest, subtle yet larger-than-life, dramatic, morally certain, inquisitive, an adventurer, hearty, conflicted between your need for privacy and your yearnings for adventure, sarcastic to hide your vulnerabilities, traditional yet progressive, kind, intuitive, visionary, reserved yet talkative, a romantic traveller, able to see the 'bigger picture', idealistic, philosophical, imaginative, emotionally reckless, sensitive yet open, in possession of a zany or dry sense of humour, optimistic, a lover of learning, inspiring, aspiring, all-embracing, playful, affectionate, gregarious, socially concerned, good-humoured, expressive yet shy, broad-minded, expansive, and guided by reason *and* emotion.

Sun/Moon Harmony Rating ★ *7 out of 10*

♑ **With the Moon in CAPRICORN,** Sun in Cancer, you are likely to be ★ Dependable, tenacious, strong-minded, patient, determined, a gentle disciplinarian, steadfast, authoritative, resourceful, committed, driven to succeed, ambitious, responsible, dedicated, considerate, critical, reserved, withdrawn, cool, organised, down-to-Earth, efficient, reliable, serious, sensual, a good leader, hard-headed but soft-hearted, sensible, reflective, materialistic, security-seeking, introverted, in possession of a good business sense, a firm but tender parent, closed off from others when hurt, understanding of practical applications and wisdom, economical, personally honourable, overly-strict on self and others, fearless, uptight, socially rigid, self-contained, capable, caring, dutiful, devoted to family, pragmatic yet sensitive, perceptive, intensely loyal, purposeful, a natural counsellor, diplomatic, compassionate, wise, helpful, concerned, and intuitively shrewd.

Sun/Moon Harmony Rating ★ *8 out of 10*

♒ **With the Moon in AQUARIUS,** Sun in Cancer, you are likely to be ★ Torn between independence and co-dependence, friendly, idealistic, emotionally detached, compassionate, nurturing of your 'brothers', protective of the underdog, whole-hearted, visionary, unconventional, paradoxical, feeling *and* thinking, imaginative, sympathetic to the human condition, honest, loyal, shrewd, faithful, original, progressive yet nostalgic, encouraging, attracted to eccentric characters, acutely aware of human need, thoughtful, living an unusual family lifestyle in some way, nurturing to many, emotionally naïve, over-identifying with causes, dedicated to group causes, attached to friends, unorthodox, impractical, humanitarian, committed to your ideals, emotionally intelligent, and ruled by your mind *and* your heart.

Sun/Moon Harmony Rating ★ *7.5 out of 10*

♓ **With the Moon in PISCES,** Sun in Cancer, you are likely to be ★ Sensitive, wallowing, adaptable, elusive, highly imaginative, intuitive, mystical, dreamy, a chaser of spiritual rainbows, good-natured, shy, easily hurt, kind-hearted, emotional, sentimental, gentle, accepting, understanding, vulnerable, gullible, trusting, private, hidden, poetic, impressionable, insightful, nurturing, receptive, creative, forgiving, retiring, withdrawn, self-sacrificing, empathetic, prone to drifting and wasting time in daydreams, easily swayed, impractical, evasive, psychic, perceptive, romantic, whimsical, charitable, blowing with the wind, reflective, and aware of the needs of others.

Sun/Moon Harmony Rating ★ *7.5 out of 10* **

** If your Moon is in Scorpio or Pisces, your Sun and Moon will form what is known in astrology as a trine aspect. This aspect is the easiest, most flowing and harmonious astrological aspect, ensuring that your Sun and Moon, or spirit and soul, are well integrated. With both luminaries in Water signs, this gives them the best possible degree of complementary energy - a blending of the elements suggests a balanced expression of personality. One drawback of the trine aspect lies in the fact that its easy flow can be *too* harmonious; if our path is too smooth and difficulties don't arise to challenge us from time to time, we can often become lazy and complacent, stunting our growth and spiritual evolution. As Water signs, you share the art of sensitivity, creativity, intrigue, compassion, a nurturing instinct, poetry, understanding, spirituality, a deep need for connection and merging with others, but may be overly sensitive, illogical, clingy, impractical, too emotional, irrational, dependent, manipulative and elusive.

YOUR BODY & HEALTH

"A physician without a knowledge of astrology has
no right to call himself a physician."
Hippocrates (born c. 460 BC)

Hippocrates, the fifth century BC Greek physician and 'father of medicine' and supposed author of the Hippocratic Oath, maintained that no one should be allowed to practise medicine who had not first studied astrology. Another Greek physician, Claudius Galen, brought together a huge range of knowledge and ideas in the second century AD which dominated medical practice until the 17th century. Among his teachings was a diagnostic technique which assumed that illnesses and their treatments were affected by and governed by the phases of the Moon. For centuries, astrology was a compulsory component of medical training (and still is in some natural medicine degrees), albeit only one aspect of diagnosis and treatment.

Medical or health astrology concerns particular ways of determining and interpreting an individual's horoscope with particular reference to health issues - diagnosis of current dis-eases, identification of areas of bodily weaknesses, and the prescription of natural cures and remedies. In ancient times, and still even today, the movement of the stars and planets was believed to affect bodily functions, and to cause ailments, or cure them.

During the Middle Ages, many drawings of the 'zodiac man' were made, which showed which signs of the zodiac were related to each part of the body, providing information as to the best times of the year to undertake cures for ailments affecting the corresponding body parts.

Health astrology persists today in many forms and among astrologers themselves, from whom clients seek counsel on health-related issues, and while it certainly cannot be used diagnose a condition or dis-ease, one's Sun sign, along with other factors of the natal chart, can definitely indicate potential problem areas of weakness or possible troubles. This branch of astrology has been found to be surprisingly accurate in most cases. While mostly accurate, none of the following information should ever be used as a substitute for professional medical advice should you be personally concerned about any of the conditions or afflictions listed for your Sun sign.

CANCERIAN HEALTH

"No other sign is so prone to let negative thoughts bring on illness, yet no other sign can create such miracles of self-healing. It's a strange contradiction, and it would immensely benefit all Cancerians to ponder it."
Linda Goodman

Cancer is associated with the Stomach, Breasts, Lacteal Ducts, Fluidic and Lymphatic Systems, Membranes, Pancreas, Diaphragm, Womb, Chest, Elbows, Thoracic Duct, Blood Serum, and the Alimentary Canal. It also governs the higher organs of digestion.

Cancer represents the energy of enfolding and containment. Your nature is cold, moist and nourishing, and principal rulerships, as well as those stated previously, include hollow and round organs such as the stomach, breasts, uterus, pericardium, synovial capsules of joints, vertebral discs, upper lobes of the liver, gall bladder, salivary glands and the chest cavity.

The most common accidents to which Cancerians are liable are chest injuries and broken ribs, while their most frequent ailments are ulcers, rheumatism, all complaints involving excess fluids and mucous congestion (such as pneumonia and bronchitis), and all diseases of the stomach and female uterine system. You are naturally inclined to over-indulge in food, with consequent indigestion.

Worry can cause Cancerian ailments - emotional stress is a Cancerian's most potent enemy - and will usually manifest in mental health issues such as melancholia and depression, or physical complaints to do with the abdomen, breast area or uterus. Sunshine is extremely therapeutic for your sign, as it lifts despondency as well as dries up any mucous-related conditions.

Typical illnesses often arise from the upper digestive tract, such as catarrh, anaemia, low energy levels, coughs and indigestion. Flatulence, obesity, contraction of the diaphragm due to panic attacks, and liver complaints are also conditions to watch for. Cancerians may also be vulnerable to eating disorders. Menstrual issues and disorders in females, such as endometriosis, troublesome periods and fluid retention, may be a problem, and you may also suffer from hypochondria or psychosomatic illnesses, which are brought on purely by your tendency to be anxious or overly emotionally sensitive. In fact, of all the zodiac signs you are the most susceptible to psychosomatic conditions, as stress and tension can have a most deleterious physical effect on you. This tendency can both put you off food, and make you irritable and complaining, or it can create an insatiable appetite which can lead to emotional or comfort-eating, digestive problems, and/or weight gain. But just as you can literally 'think' yourself sick, so too can you think your way to recovery and good health. But you are one patient who should not be indulged with too much sympathy, as it's too easy for you to lapse into self-pity.

Keeping the sensitive Cancerian system in good order requires regular, rhythmical exercise. Swimming from as early an age as possible, as well as dancing, are recommended. You are likely to suffer digestive complaints, particularly when worried. The lymphatic and sympathetic nervous system are particular areas that may prove vulnerable, as well as the ovaries and uterus.

Disorders affecting the liver and pancreas are prevalent amongst those born under the sign of the Crab, and because both your ruler the Moon and your zodiac sign rules over mucous membranes, these are areas which are also prone to illness or adverse conditions.

It must be emphasised that the sign Cancer has nothing to do with the dis-ease of the same name. However, because Cancer rules the breasts, women of this sign should ensure they regularly examine them and have periodic medical check-ups regarding this area.

Cancer rules the Solar Plexus chakra that highly sensitive nervous 'centre' in the abdomen commonly referred to as 'the pit of the stomach'. If you are a typical Cancerian, it is here that you will feel a constant play of emotions, making your stomach churn. It is here - not your brain - that you first register what is going on around you, and as a result, your digestion can be frequently upset.

The vitality of Cancerian people is naturally quite low, but can be encouraged through regular exercise and a strong, healthy diet.

Cancer people are not usually robust in youth and seem to catch more than their share of childhood illnesses. Your recuperative powers may also be somewhat weak, and chronic ailments prevalent. Once you reach adulthood, your delicate constitution may gather more physical strength and you are likely to live to a fine old age.

Your ruler, the Moon, also bears an influence on your health. The Moon governs Body Fluids, Mucous Membranes, Blood, the Lymphatic System, Stomach, Breasts, Womb, Ovaries, Bladder, Oesophagus, Synovial Fluid, the whole Alimentary System, the Senses of Taste and Sight (left eye in males, right eye in females), and the left-hand side of the body. The Moon has always been considered a fruitful celestial body, encouraging reproduction and the nurturing care of children through the flow of maternal instinct. The Moon governs functional ailments rather than organic ones. It has been said that overall health is best when the natal Moon is in a negative/feminine sign.

Keeping yourself in excellent health overall, with a special awareness of Cancer's vulnerable points, is key to achieving all you set out to do, and getting the most out of your life!

THE CELL SALTS ★ ASTROLOGICAL TONICS

Homeopathy and astrology have colluded to provide a wonderful list of astrological tonics, one particularly suited to each of the twelve signs. These are called 'homeopathic cell salts', 'tissue salts' or 'biochemic cell salts', and are available in most health food stores, are inexpensive and easy to take. They are considered to be gentle, effective and safe, even for children, people in fragile health states, and the elderly. Although the full picture, drawn from a full natal horoscope, gives a fuller, more accurate idea of an individual's unique constitution, even simply working with one's date of birth can be enough for the medical astrologer to suggest the use of a cell salt based upon the correlation with an individual's Sun sign. As well as the cell salts having a significant effect upon physical ailments, they can also profoundly influence the subtle energy bodies, including the mental, emotional, etheric and spiritual. Although the most common use of these salts is based upon each salt's correspondence with a Sun sign, use of the cell salt related to one's Moon sign can assist with addressing deeper underlying emotional issues, such as anxiety, depression, panic and fear. Use of the cell salt relating to your Moon sign will therefore help to restore your sense of safety, balance, security and emotional resilience. In the first seven years of life, when the Moon is the most influential sphere in our lives, Lunar cell salts are the most appropriate choice as a remedy or tonic.

For specific health problems, take both the salt of your Sun or Moon sign, *and* the salt that pertains to the specific condition. The same principle applies to the Ascendant sign, as the First House represents one's physical health, and especially if the Sun or Moon is a rising planet, which means rulership of the whole chart. For the purposes of this book, however, the cell salt that correlates with your Sun sign only is outlined.

TISSUE SALT FOR CANCER ★ CALC FLUOR.

Calcaria Fluorica, or Calc Fluor. (Calcium fluoride) is the cell salt for Cancer. Found mainly in the bones, teeth, nerves and muscles, Calc Fluor. is especially needed in a potent form in the brain, heart, lungs, kidneys, eyelid, bone covers, muscles and ligaments, as it is necessary where elasticity of the tissue is required for proper functioning. This tissue salt enables the fibres to stretch and then return to their original form. As this mineral salt is an important constituent of bone cover and tooth enamel, it has a profound effect on the skeletal growth and dental development of children. And for this reason, Calc Fluor. should be taken *before* any signs of damage or disorder appear. Pregnant and nursing mothers could also pass on these benefits to their offspring by supplementing with Calc Fluor. An important component of the hard tissues and elastic fibres of the body, such as those found in the veins, glands, teeth, skin, blood vessels, bones, nails, lens of the eye and muscles, this cell salt attends to restoring the connective tissues. Deficiency of this cell salt can result in loss of tissue elasticity, dental problems, malnutrition of the bones, or loss of elasticity, resulting in hardness. As Cancer rules the stomach, breasts, mucous membranes and bodily fluids, Calc Fluor. provides nourishment and the flexibility needed for optimum functioning of these areas. It maintains supple breast and abdominal tissues, as well as restoring resilience to 'boggy' or fissured mucous membranes. One significant use of this tissue salt is for the alleviating of the symptoms of emphysema. In this condition, the lung's air sacs cannot stretch or compress enough to enable the person to breathe properly, and over time, in conjunction with other natural therapies, Calc Fluor. can help to correct this malfunction. This mineral salt can be found in foods such as rye, grapes, pumpkin, cabbage, oranges and lemons.

WATER SIGN CANCER & THE PHLEGMATIC HUMOUR

Greek physician Hippocrates (460 - 370 BC) theorised that certain human behaviours were caused by body fluids, called 'humours'. Later, Galen of Pergamon (AD 131 - 200), a Greek physician, developed the first typology of temperaments to encompass many facets of the human psyche and physiology. These also related to the classical elements of Fire, Earth, Air and Water - as choleric, melancholic, sanguine and phlegmatic respectively. According to the Greeks who developed the temperament theory (the word stems from the Latin word *temperamentum*, meaning mixture), temperament is the 'mixture' of qualities that combine to form elements in physics and humours in medicine. The Greeks sought equilibrium in the four qualities of hot, cold, wet (moist), and dry, the elements of Earth, Air, Fire and Water, and the four humours of choler or yellow bile, melancholer or black bile, blood and phlegm. If balance was achieved, the person was said to be well- or even-tempered, and the importance of determining the temperament allowed for imbalances to be treated.

In ancient times, each of the four types of humours corresponded to a different personality type, which were associated with a domination of various biological functions. It was suggested that the temperaments came to clearest manifestation in childhood, between around the ages of six and fourteen of age, after which they become subordinate, but still influential, factors in our personality. It is important to note that your temperament is not your personality. However, your personality can incorporate parts of the temperament in its expression. Personality is shaped by both external and internal factors, whereas the temperament is innate, an inborn, inherent part of each individual.

For Water, the humour is phlegmatic, and it is characterised by a longer response-delay, but short-lived response. Generally low in drive and motivation, phlegmatic natives seek to preserve low energy stores. Phlegmatic types usually give the impression of being calm, naïve and simple, longing for peace in the soul.

Generally inward, people with this temperament tend to be private, reasonable, patient, caring, thoughtful, passive, sluggish, content, and tolerant, have a rich inner life, and seek quiet, peaceful environments. Being impressionable, phlegmatic types are often 'awakened' by others' interests in a subject. Steadfast, placid, controlled, reliable, even-tempered, consistent in their habits, they make steady and loyal friends. Your speech may be slow or hesitant, and you may appear clumsy or ponderous. On a physical level, the home of this humour is in the veins and lymphatics, and this humour nourishes the body on a deep and fundamental level.

A phlegmatic disposition represents a slow, even temperament. Its taste is sweet, its nature alkaline, its indication phlegm. The phlegmatic humour is connected with the *liquid* ^ body, and is traditionally associated with cold and wet conditions.

^ A couple of thousand years ago, the Mesopotamians, Chinese and Egyptians, and more recently the Arabs, practised a medicine called 'of three bodies'. According to the doctors of the ancient world (who often practised as astrologers as well), a human being had three bodies: the physical body, the ethereal (or vital) body and the astral body, imparting a holistic approach to health. In modern medicine, usually only the physical body is focused upon fully. According to tradition, this physical body comprises three principles or states corresponding to three primordial elements: *solid* (Earth), *liquid* (Water) and *gas* (Air). This is the material body, the physical outer cover of muscles, nerves and organs held together by the skeleton. The Fire element corresponds with the *astral* body, which sits outside the physical body in one's auric field.

MONEY ATTRIBUTES

Colour for Increased Earning Power ★ Silver

The following plants can be used by all zodiac signs to assist in attracting money ★ Ginger, Allspice, Clover, Orange, Marjoram, Cinnamon, Sassafras, Woodruff, Bergamot, Tonka Beans, Heliotrope, Alfalfa, Coltsfoot, Thyme, Mace, Irish Moss, Clove, Almond, Corn, Honeysuckle, Sesame, Nutmeg, Vetiver, Poppy, Jasmine, Dill and Elder Flower. To attract luck and success, try using any of the above, combined with any of the following: Alfalfa Seeds, Basil, Mustard Seeds, Vervain Leaves, Poppy Seeds, Rosemary, Lemon, Anise and Holly.

Striving for financial gain and abundance with a healthy inner moral compass is, in my view, one of the most noble of goals we can set for ourselves. When we have more money, we are better placed to help ourselves and of course others; after all, as Abraham Maslow's Hierarchy of Needs model (1943) attests, once our primary and base survival needs have been satisfied, we can then advance higher towards loftier achievements, such as self-confidence, creativity and self-actualisation. Prosperity allows us to turn our attention to these more transcendental matters - to reach for lives not just of material comfort and luxuries, but of meaning, generosity, balance, harmony, fulfilment and joy. Our Sun sign can offer clues as to how we go about acquiring, earning, saving, maintaining, and allowing the overall flow of giving and receiving money. What's *your* money style?

"No one is a more capable manager of funds than the Crab. He's an expert at accumulating cash and making it grow ... it will seldom dwindle in his tenacious hands or run through his shrewd fingers, and you won't catch him tossing bundles of it out the window for the sheer joy of it."
Linda Goodman

Being ruled by the changeable and fluctuating Moon, Cancerians may experience many ups and downs with income. Also, being comprised of primal female energy, any legacies or inheritances you receive are likely to come from your mother or female relatives. Cancerians are good at keeping hold of money and you are careful in your investments and purchases, being shrewd in all your financial decisions, and have a natural aversion to taking risks.

Being security-oriented, you like to build a nest egg. Although you have a flair for business, you rarely trust others, so financial affairs are usually self-managed. You are cautious and love the security that money can provide you. You can cling to it too tightly, however, and this may come across as mean or greedy. Accused though you may be of meanness, you are generous with loved ones.

There is one word that describes you perfectly - dependable. One of the reasons for this is again that pressing desire for security. However, it is important to remember that you are a leader and quite the genius at achieving not only stability in your-self, but in your financial situation as well. You are gifted with the happy knack of making money, and the even more joyful facility of hanging onto it.

Because you are a Cardinal sign you are full of enterprise, and even though you may be content to sit back in comfort while learning your trade of choice, it won't be long before your amazing memory and ability to adapt to your surroundings will enable you to make considerable progress - and money!

Your financial situation will usually be fairly secure, albeit mildly fluctuating, as extravagance is not in your make-up. You understand the value of money and hate to see it wasted, especially if it has taken hard work or familial sacrifices to earn it. Your need for a solid, stable domestic situation sees you saving with gusto towards a home to call your very own, for you also like to possess in every sense of the word.

You have a basic underlying insecurity that attracts you to money, because it buys those things that bring you inner peace. You have an instinctive understanding of money matters, and using your shrewd, intuitive and imaginative powers, you can come up with ingenious ways of making it - and perhaps even more importantly, keeping it!

COLOURS

Chromatomancy, or divination by colour, is a form of energy therapy that has been used for thousands of years by many different cultures. It works on the principle that we make both instinctive and rational choices or preferences based on circumstances which are already present in ourselves; colour also has an effect on the energy in an environment, and we in turn respond consciously or subconsciously to our surroundings. If we look at the causes, and try to understand the reasons, as to why we are so receptive to one particular colour over another, we will see that there is a subtle link between certain hues and our emotional and instinctive individual reactions. The colour which we give to things results from a combination of three elements:

1. The light or the vibration of a body;

2. The context in which it is found and the interaction between its own light and that of its environment;

3. The sensitivity of the eye's retina which sees the body in question. Because of this, a colour can vary, depending on the individual's perceptions, namely, his sensitivity, his mood, and his view of reality. For a long time, people have understood that their vision of reality depends a lot on their moods, feelings and emotions.

Chromatotherapy, or colour healing, stems from this body of evidence, and its main application is the use of colours for healing purposes. Colours are generally associated with characteristics, feelings, stones, metals, plants and flowers, planets and even the zodiac signs. In varying cultures, they play a significant role in ceremonies and regalia.

We vibrate to the frequency of colour, shown through its continual movement and change in our aura ^. One of the most beautiful examples of colour is the rainbow. This architect of colour is caused by the refraction and internal reflection of light in raindrops. Colour can be perceived as either a pigment, or as illumination. The colour spectrum can be divided into eight main colours: red, orange, yellow, green, turquoise, blue, violet and magenta. Each colour has a wavelength and frequency that carry different therapeutic qualities which have indirect effects upon our health and bodily systems, and because of this, coupled with the fact that we as living energy centres emanate colour, colour can be a great medium in healing, calming, energising, increasing and attracting.

Aristotle, in the fourth century BCE, considered blue and yellow to be the true primary colours and related them to life's polarities: Sun and Moon, male and female, stimulation and sedation, in and out, expansion and contraction. He also associated colours with the four elements of Fire, Earth, Air and Water. Hippocrates, the father of medicine, used colour extensively in medicinal healing and recognised that the therapeutic effects of a white violet differed from those of a purple one. In the fifteenth century, Paracelsus placed particular importance on the role of colour in healing.

Each Sun sign and planetary body has a specific colour or colours which when used in combination with wishing rituals, can enhance their power immensely. Coloured candles can be used to good effect, as the fire energy of the flame/s increases the power of any wish, and flames are also a useful aid to meditating on, focusing upon or clarifying what you want. Coloured candles help to focus the energy for whatever purpose the colour is in sympathy with (e.g. green for money, pink for romance, orange for joy, etc.)

With all this in mind, wearing or using your Sun sign or ruling planet's magical colour/s on a regular basis will undoubtedly bring great benefits.

^ The aura is defined as an energy field, which interpenetrates with, and radiates beyond, the physical body. Clairvoyantly seen, the aura is full of light, colour and shade. The trained healer or seer sees or senses indications within the aura as to the spiritual, physical and emotional state of the individual. Much of the auric colour and energy emanates from the chakras.

YOUR LUCKY COLOURS

For Cancer ★ White, Silver, Emerald Green, Smoky Grey, Silvery Grey, Pastel Shades, Glistening Whites, Opalescent and Iridescent Hues

For The Moon ★ Silver, Dark Blue, Violet, White, Cream, Nondescript Colours

With the sign of the Crab, the first Water sign, the zodiac reaches the end of the first series of elements. The shy but determined Cancerian feels happiest in silvery blues, silvers, shimmery whites and smoky greys.

Each of the eight colours of the rainbow spectrum also has a complementary colour to which it is matched. Red is complementary to turquoise, orange to blue, yellow to violet, and green to magenta. If these colour pairs enhance each other's most spellbinding qualities and energies, perhaps you could try wearing your Sun sign's lucky colour with its matching complementary colour in order to produce extra magical results! Your lucky Cancerian colours are white, silver and violet, which complements yellow. Now you know your colours, you can dress for success!

FEATURE COLOURS ★
WHITE, VIOLET & SILVER

★ WHITE ★

Healing Qualities ★ Purity, Grace, Innocence, Peace, Harmony, Transcendence, Calming, Spirituality, Cleansing. Because white contains all colours, it can be utilised for all magical and healing purposes.

Keywords ★ The Soul (white light), Innocence, Purity, Naiveté, Faith, Peace, Cleanliness, Sincerity, Truth, the Higher Self

White is actually not a single colour, but is a synthesis of all the colours. As such it combines the qualities of *all* colours. White is the 'colour' most closely associated with spirituality and purity. It is often associated with Divinity and as such can also represent the element of spirit. Symbolising the planetary energies of Pluto, it can be used for blessings, healing, wisdom, chastity, innocence and truth. Through nature, white has gained some important associations: purity (the purity of glistening snow for example), elegance and grace (perhaps originating from the gentle movements of white swans gliding across still water), a symbol of innocence (perhaps owing to its untinged, untainted appearance), and peace and harmony (the white dove is a universally-recognised symbol of these). The colour white abounds in nature, but its presence is usually elusive, difficult to access or short-lived, making us appreciate it all the more. Examples of this are clouds, snow, polar bears, white seals, doves, salt mines, crystal caves, glaciers, mountain peaks, the state of 'white heat' of an object, and white foaming water.

In the material world, pharmaceutical companies use white as the colour for their tablets because of the association it has with healing; and in many religions, leaders wear white to indicate that they are representatives of a Divine authority. Many religious celebrations and traditions feature white as the predominant colour, such as that worn by the bride in weddings in many cultures to symbolise faith and sacraments, white being used to symbolise the magical fifth element of ether in Paganism, white being linked to the Chinese forces of yang which represent masculinity, and Buddhism's 'Lotus of Enlightenment'. Spiritual agents are also associated with 'heavenly white', especially guardian angels who are often seen bathed in a white luminescent light complete with the traditional white wings. Ghosts are also depicted as white beings, and vampires and zombies are often depicted with white or pale skin to indicate that they are no longer beings of this world but rather belong in the spiritual realms. White beings include: Vivien, Merlin, Aguane, Nymphs, Chinese White Dragons, Cerridwen and Deva. Further, white is the most reported colour from near-death experiences. Those who have encountered these, often tell of leaving their bodies and being able to view themselves from a remote location, which is usually accompanied by a movement upwards through a long tunnel as they are drawn towards a strong white light which reportedly emanates profound sensations of love, serenity, peace and happiness. Psychics believe that all living things possess an energy field surrounding their bodies called an aura, and by reading this a psychic can discern that being's wellbeing. If the colour white is present it usually means that they are deeply spiritual and can indicate the influence of Divine agents such as heavenly angels or spirit guides. White is also the colour linked with travelling into the astral world through the art of projection.

★ VIOLET ★

Planetary Association ★ The Moon, Neptune

Complementary Colour ★ Yellow

Violet is the most spiritual colour in the spectrum, the one most likely to trigger mental relaxation and meditation, and so is well suited to sensitive, deep-thinking, meditative and introspective types, or those who wish to incorporate these qualities into their character. Its healing powers are believed to benefit the entire nervous and cerebral systems. Although it is very calming, working with it may leave you feeling ungrounded and 'spaced out', so balancing this out with the grounding energies of red, black or brown energy might help. The colour of violet pertains to spirituality, dignity, insight, inspiration and self-respect.

Violet is a wonderful tonic for those who don't trust their own thoughts or who are unable to love themselves. Various shades of violet have been associated with mystery, magic and the occult. It is a colour which can lift the receptive person into a higher state of consciousness, and can lead one into a realm of spiritual awareness where a gateway awaits, that passes through into a garden of being united with one's true self and Divine inner being. Violet (and all shades of purple in general) is regarded as a highly spiritual colour and is the colour for those seeking Divine fulfilment and nourishment. Violet represents the future, the imagination and dreams, and inspires and enhances psychic enlightenment and abilities. It teaches us to trust our inner flow, and also our intuitive and creative expressions. It is associated with the Crown chakra, linking it with higher wisdom, helping to connect us with greater cosmic awareness and sacred consciousness. Interestingly, this colour is found at the end of the spectrum, and when it extends a bit further it becomes ultra-violet, disappearing into the wide, unknowable ether.

★ SILVER ★

Planetary Association ★ The Moon

Healing Qualities ★ Happiness, Prosperity, Prestige, Opulence, Wisdom, Purging Negativity, Luck, Femininity, Purifying

Keywords ★ Channelling, Clairvoyance, Astral Energies, Moon, Silver Birch, Amulets, Wisdom

The colour of the Moon, silver can be used for astral or dream work, practising scrying (crystal ball gazing or divination) and for wish magic. Because of its associations with the Moon, silver is also connected with femininity and feminine power. Silver has been revered as a mystical metal since the dawn of civilisation. Ancient alchemists regarded it to be especially valuable and attempted to transmute other metals to produce it *. They used the symbol of the Moon to represent this metal (identified in the Periodic Table of Elements as 'Ag'), which they named 'luna'. Silver, being linked with the Third Eye chakra, is useful for channelling energy, both of a psychic nature and, in more practical terms, of electricity and heat. Silver has also come to represent quality, class and style, as the expressions 'silver service' and 'born with a silver spoon in mouth' exemplify. It also embodies the wisdom gained by learning through experience and optimism, through questing for a 'silver lining' in the face of life's adversities. Mirrors are flat silver-coloured surfaces that reflect all light. Since medieval times, mirrors have been used by clairvoyants and other diviners to make contact with mystical spirits and foretell the future, back then leading to the belief that parallel worlds were hidden behind mirrors, something which Lewis Carroll's literary Alice explores in her *Through the Looking Glass* adventures.

When people and some animals grow older, their hair loses its original colour and turns silver. Someone who is older is more likely to have more knowledge, which is why the colour silver also relates to wisdom. Chinese Feng Shui is based on the principles of the five elements. Silver is a strong metallic element and as such has powerful Chi qualities. According to theory, it can be used to support the Water element, but destroys Wood. Another potent silver association is that in heraldry, metallic silver paint is called argent. The word 'argent' inspired the country name Argentina, because the first European explorers reported seeing a huge silver mountain there. Silver overall corresponds with that which is of material value, versatility, liveliness and higher levels of consciousness.

* Alchemists believed that mercury was the substance used in creation. They thought that this element was a particular type of silver which is why they called mercury 'quicksilver'.

Violet, and its complementary rainbow spectrum colour yellow, and white and silver, are Cancer's special LUCKY colours! The two can be worn or otherwise used together to dazzling and mesmerising effect.

CANCER'S CHAKRA CORRESPONDENCE
★ SACRAL

The word 'chakra' comes from the Sanskrit and means 'wheel', disc' or 'circle'. Chakras are vitally important to your physical health, emotional wellbeing and spiritual growth, and are regarded as a complete integrated system that works holistically. The chakras are funnel-shaped spinning energy vortexes of multicoloured light. These swirling vortexes of energy absorb and distribute life-force, the subtle energy known as *prana*. The seven master chakras - Root, Sacral, Solar Plexus, Heart, Throat, Third Eye and Crown - lie in the centre line of the body, with the first five embedded within the spinal column. Each chakra vibrates at a different vibrational frequency and on a different note, and responds to specific life issues or 'thought forms'.

The lower body chakras deal with physical issues. As we move up the body, the chakras correspond to increasingly spiritual concerns. As a consequence, each chakra's energy vibrates at a different rate, depending on whether they govern earthbound or ethereal issues. The lower chakras have slower and denser vibrations, while the higher chakras spin at faster speeds with higher vibrations.

Because the chakras have no physical manifestation and cannot be located using any scientific instrument, they have tended to be viewed with scepticism by many Western medical professionals, a distinction they share with energy points in acupuncture and the notion of meridians. Instead, they are believed to have been sensed intuitively by many people over many centuries, and indeed people in yoga positions and in deep meditation have reported experiencing the sensation of a surge of energy rising from the base of the spine and emerging through the top of the head. Some people have even said they have seen points of blue light when their *kundalini* energy has risen from the lowest chakra to the highest, as well as experiencing a profound sense of happiness and ecstasy.

In summary, the Universal Life Force enters the body through the Crown chakra at the top of the head. As it works its way through the body, it flows through the other centres. As it spreads to the Base chakra, it is said to arouse the kundalini energy, which yogis believe sleeps in a coiled serpentine form.

The chakra associated with Cancer is the second, or Sacral chakra, which governs sexual, physical, material and creative desires and expressions.

SACRAL CHAKRA

Location ★ Below the Navel
Colour ★ Orange
Concerned with ★ Physical, Sexual, Creative & Material Desires

Gland ★ Cells of Leydig *
Essential Oils ★ Carrot Seed, Dill, Geranium, Jasmine, Hyssop, Neroli, Marjoram, Sandalwood, Rose
Animals ★ Sea Creatures
Shape ★ Light Blue Crescent
Element ★ Water
Planets ★ Moon, Pluto
Zodiac Signs ★ Cancer, Scorpio
Flower ★ Six-petalled Lotus
Energy State ★ Liquid
Mantra ★ VAM

* The Sacral chakra regulates what are called the 'cells of Leydig', which are testicular or ovarian cells that produce and secrete testosterone.

Positive Expression ★ Balanced, creative, personally vital

Negative Expression (Blockage) ★ Imbalanced, over- or undersexed, inflexible, emotionally cold, low energy, low libido, inhibiting, difficulty changing, difficulty experiencing joy, hyper-emotional, overly focused on physical pleasures

The Sacral chakra is located around the sexual organ region. Its Sanskrit name is *svadhisthana*, and its symbol is a six-petalled orange lotus flower containing a second lotus flower and an upward-pointing crescent Moon in a white circle. Balance in this chakra is expressed as originality, creativity and vitality. It corresponds to the sex glands and the sacral nerve plexus. Crystals that can be used to cleanse and balance this chakra are mostly orange stones, including: Carnelian, Amber, Orange Calcite, Citrine, Golden Labradorite (Orange Sunstone), Topaz, Tangerine Quartz and Thulite.

LUCKY CAREER TIPS & PATHS THAT WILL MAKE YOUR BANK BALANCE & SPIRITUAL SELF SOAR

The branch of astrology known as 'vocational astrology' encompasses the areas of one's calling, career path, or ideal profession. Careers, jobs, professions and occupations can all mean different things to different people, but to simplify the definition, I refer to a vocation as one's true calling, one's authentic path, and a dynamic way of life which pays an income in some form and leads to a deep fulfilment of personal and spiritual needs. An ideal vocation will provide self-fulfilment, ego satisfaction, and feed one's inner drive to achieve what they ultimately wish to achieve, whether that be to gain recognition, wealth or approval, to travel, to learn and fulfil an inner need for knowledge, an urge to serve others in some way, or an urge to improve personal, societal or Universal conditions.

In order to gain ultimate fulfilment and self-esteem, we all need a purpose in life. Many people gain this through their work, providing the job or career they choose suits their temperament, talents and aspirations. If our professional life is unsatisfactory or disharmonious in any way, frustration, unhappiness and even despair can result. Although your whole horoscope would need to be drawn up and interpreted in order to gain more substantial, deeper insights into your ideal career and purpose, you can begin by being guided by your Sun sign, which can give you many pointers to a suitable, and therefore successful, career path. You just never know, something in the following might jump out at you and make your soul dance immediately - and hopefully all the way to the bank!

With your Sun in Cancer, you are emotional, loving, feeling, protective, nurturing and needy, but also shrewd and clever in business. Being of the Water element and ruled by the Moon, you are sensitive and it is second nature to you to care deeply about others. Although you possess a soft and tender character, you also have a very tenacious streak, so once you decide on a particular goal or line of work, you will persevere until it is achieved; once you commit yourself to a specific career path, you usually stick with it and give it all you've got. It is in this way that you can be tough, enterprising and inflexible.

In a broad sense, Cancer is the most suited to domestic work, such as housework, cleaning, caring, and running and organising the domestic, familial front. After all, Cancer and the Fourth House rule the home and family, so you have an instinctive knack of knowing how to maintain the home and hearth - both others' and your own. You also like to be in and look at homes themselves, so you may enjoy a career in real estate, property, working from home in some capacity, the building industry, interior design, or house renovations.

Your natural desire to care for and nurture other people would be an invaluable asset for occupations involving the care of children or the elderly, nursing, counselling, housekeeping, missionary work, and many other avenues which give you the opportunity to help others.

Cancer is also related to nutrition and all aspects of the food and beverage industries, so suitable professions might be in the fields of naturopathy, dietetics, restaurants, food stores, and cooking (especially from home).

Because you are a naturally protective, conservative and cautious person, you would also be well-equipped for any type of career which involves managing or handling money, and although reticent and quite shy, you have a surprisingly good head for business and enterprise.

Your strong sense of heritage, history, roots, origins and nostalgia would make you a great Antiques Dealer, Collector of Nostalgia, Historian, Museum Curator, or Family History Consultant.

The following fields and positions may hold appeal for your feeling, caring, determined, family-and-home-oriented spirit, and are suitable for Cancerians overall: Work-From-Home, Chef/Cook, Social Worker, Hotelier, Elderly or Child Welfare Officer, Family Counsellor, Commerce, Landscape Designer, Caterer, Midwife, Governess, Nanny, Laundry Work, Nursing, In-Home Care, Childcare, Family Day Care, Palliative Care, and Supplying Domestic Needs.

Above all, you seek shelter, protection, comfort, peace and security, and so may stay in the same job for fear of the unknown or because it becomes so comfortable that you rely on its reliability and sameness. This, coupled with your need for financial stability in order to provide for your loved ones and dependants, makes you a solid, dependable worker in any field you choose to undertake.

LUCKY PLACES WHERE YOUR ENERGY IS HEIGHTENED

As the Water element and phlegmatic humour corresponds with cold and moist conditions, cool, damp, rainy places suit your constitution, disposition and temperament. The following nations, countries and cities are also places whose vibrations are closely allied with the sign of Cancer: Mauritius, Comoros Islands, United States, Paraguay, New Zealand, Mexico, Scotland, Canada, the Netherlands (Amsterdam), Turkey (Istanbul), Italy (Venice), Burundi, Cayman Islands, Rhodesia and New York City. The Bahamas, Rwanda, Cape Verde Islands, Malawi, Iraq, Laos, The Seychelles, Venezuela, Mozambique, Slovenia, Madagascar, Liberia, Columbia, Denmark, Algeria, Solomon Islands, the Philippines, Argentina, Somalia, the Wallis and Futuna Islands, and Vietnam are other places connected with Cancerians. Anywhere peaceful near or on water, and cellars are also in tune with the Cancerian energy, as are romantic and family-oriented places. A country-style stay at a French vineyard that is run by a long line of a generational family, a dreamy boat ride in Venice, being wined and dined on any waterfront, walking alongside the canals of Amsterdam, attending a Full Moon festival, a stroll along the River Seine, a day viewing beautiful art in a quiet gallery, climbing the Eiffel Tower with your beloved, or a holiday spent by the humble ocean collecting crabs and frolicking with your family, could all very well be your ticket to Cancerian heaven!

GEMS & CRYSTALS

"People love stones, and apparently stones love people. Like the angels they may be, they seem endlessly willing to serve the wellbeing of humans and to help us achieve our desires ...Unlike people of the ancient past, we now have access to virtually the entire mineral kingdom. We have the opportunity to work like modern alchemists, combining and arranging the stones and their currents, looking for combinations and patterns that can help us enhance our inner and outer lives."

Robert Simmons, *Stones of the New Consciousness*

Each crystal and mineral of the Earth embodies different qualities, patterns or potential expressions of the Divine language, the silent whispers of the Universe. If we can accept the fact that the human body is a sophisticated, multi-faceted antenna system comprised of a crystalline matrix that is constantly transmitting and receiving all manner of energies, it could then be assumed that energy and body workers who use quartz, shells and stones, which are also crystalline materials, have the power to promote resonant interactions with the liquid 'crystal' structures found in human tissues. It could even be said that we are all made of essentially the same substances and structures, and that crystals and gemstones vibrate at varying energetic levels which can connect with our own in order to 'buzz' and dance together to make a harmonious Uni-verse both within and without.

All crystals work through vibrational balancing and by channelling energy. The magic of crystals is in their colour, which is determined by the rate at which their atoms vibrate; these vibrations can be matched to the energy given by your own body's aura. And just as light can be focused and refracted through gemstones, so too can all kinds of psychic energy, from healing energies to Divine communications.

Gemstones can help us attune to higher vibrations and bring them into our own experience and being. This theory of crystal resonance suggests that the characteristic energy patterns emanated by any stone can be transferred into the 'liquid crystal medium' of our bodies through resonance. Our bodies, being composed of these tuneable liquids, can mimic and mirror any consistent vibrational pattern with which we come into contact; we can therefore resonate with the healthful qualities of various crystals and minerals.

Crystals and precious stones have been valued throughout world cultures over many centuries for their healing virtues and capacities to imbue courage, strength, invulnerability, clairvoyance, love and numerous other qualities. Wearing gemstones is one of the simplest and most effective self-healing practices you can undertake, and wearing or carrying those stones whose vibrations correspond with the qualities you wish to embody brings their energetic currents into engagement with your body.

Over time the phenomenon of energetic integration, may be felt tangibly and your own vibrational field may internalise the stone's currents and adjust to them and effectively 'store' them, making them, eventually, a part of your own vibrational make-up. And we seem to know from the resonances we feel within our bodies when in contact with these gemstones, that crystals emanate tangible, if oft immeasurable, currents.

Crystals act as transmitters and amplifiers of your will or intentions - as long as your will or intentions are in sympathy with the crystal's energy. The mineral kingdom refers to stones, minerals and crystals and the associations and vibrations they carry. When working with stones, we are working with several different layers of spiritual energies, and although they can be regarded as inanimate 'psychic batteries', they are actually moving, vibrating masses of energy which transmit potential and power into our lives. Some crystals and stones even have receptive powers, which means they can absorb energy and retain it within until cleansed or re-programmed.

Although it is untrue that the only stones you can usefully wear are the ones astrologically matched with your Sun sign or ruling planet, those which align with your Sun sign or ruling planet are your most fortuitous and therefore strongest 'attractors' and 'amplifiers'.

Twelve oracular gemstones were described in the Bible, as the author of *Exodus* (28-15 and 17-21) knew them. Yahweh spoke to Moses about the breastplate he would have to wear to train for priesthood, and described it to him in these words: "And thou shalt make the breastplate of judgement with cunning work; ... And thou shalt set in it settings of stones, even four rows of stones; the first row shall be a sardius, a topaz, and a carbuncle. And the second row shall be an emerald, a sapphire and a diamond. And the third row an opal, an agate and an amethyst. And the fourth row a beryl, and an onyx, and a jasper; they shall be set in hold in their inclosings. And the stones shall be with the children ... (all) twelve (of them)." Given that the compilers of the Bible lived during a time when astrological belief was prevalent in Babylon, it seems valid to assert that these previously named gemstones would have some astrological basis. Further, since these ancient people supposedly made correlations between each of the twelve precious stones, and one of the twelve zodiac signs, there are seven crystalline systems set down in crystallography (or the science of the laws which influence the formation, structure and geometric, physical and chemical properties of crystallised matter) as analogous with the seven traditional ruling planets of the zodiac.

However, nobody is under the rule of one planet alone. We are all in essence a complex mixture of every planet, many elements and varying aspects, depending on their positions, placements and prominence in our birth chart. Everything that goes on in the skies above us affects what is going on here on Earth, and also *within* us. Your lucky stones are to assist you to tune into your Sun sign's energy and planetary influences, but you are by no means limited to the ones listed for your sign alone. Above all, let your stones, whichever ones you choose, work for you and allow them to transport your very own unique and magical energy into the wider Universe.

> "Beautiful and strong is the material of stones, but more beautiful and much more powerful is the mystery that emanates from them."
> **Chinese Poet & Alchemist, Li Po, 8th Century A.D.**

★ CLEAR QUARTZ ★

The Master Healer ★ *For All Zodiac Signs*

A common, well-known and popular gem, clear quartz (sometimes known as rock crystal) is an all-purpose 'jack-of-all-trades' stone. It amplifies the magic of any work you do or wishes you make. It is connected with all the chakras and increases the power of all other crystals. Clear quartz is a deep soul cleanser, which unblocks and regulates energy and emotions on all levels. It is balancing and harmonising. In various cultures, quartz crystal is reputed to be the most powerful crystal, the 'grandfather crystal', and the 'chief of the Stone People'. Clear quartz is also considered to be the only gemstone that is modifiable to suit your needs *, as other crystals automatically contain and retain their own specific resonance or natural signature. In essence, clear quartz is the most easily programmable and the most overall healing and readily accessible crystals of the mineral kingdom, holding a unique importance in the Universe of gems. And because of its all-encompassing nature and wide-ranging healing abilities, it has zodiacal affinities with all the signs.

* To program your clear quartz crystal, simply hold it on your Third Eye chakra (between and just above the

physical eyes) and concentrate on the purpose for which you wish to use it. Be positive and receptive while you allow your crystal to fill with this energy. If you wish, you could also state the intention of the programming out loud, for example, 'I program this crystal for love / healing / meditation / abundance / protection or (insert your own word here)'. You could also run your clear quartz crystal under running water, allow it to dry naturally, then hold the stone with both hands, bring it up to your mouth and blow into it sharply three times in order to impregnate it with your own breath. Then, hold it firmly in one hand and silently invite and welcome it into your life as a friend, helper and guide.

CANCERIAN & LUNAR LUCKY CRYSTALS, STONES & GEMS

Cancer birth stones ★ Moonstone, Pearl, Ruby

June birth stones ★ Emerald, Pearl, Moonstone

July birth stones ★ Onyx, Ruby, Turquoise, Carnelian

Moonstone, Pearl, Ruby (your three primary birthstones), Emerald, Onyx, Turquoise and Carnelian (June and July birthstones) are your luckiest stones, and at least one of these gems should be worn about your person to ensure good luck and increase your overall magnetism. Fire Agate, Moss Agate, Dendritic Agate, Beryl, Rhodonite, Aventurine, Opal, Amber, Brown Spinel, Chrysoprase, Pink Tourmaline, Green Garnet Grossuralite, Blue Agate, White Onyx, Snowflake Obsidian, Tibetan Quartz,

Titanium Quartz, Tektite, and Calcite (green, blue and orange), also align with Cancerian energy.

CRYSTALS & THE PLANETS

All the Vedic texts agree in relating gems to planets. This verse from the *Jatax Parijat* links each gem to a planet:

*'The ruby is the gem of the Lord of the Day (the Sun),
The shining pearl is the gem of the cold Moon,
Red coral is the gem of Mars,
The emerald is the gem of noble Mercury,
Yellow sapphire is the gem of Jupiter, instructor of gods,
Diamond is the gem of Venus, instructor of demons,
Blue sapphire is the gem of Saturn.'*

Each planet influences its gem, and their curative power varies according to the position of its planet in the zodiac. Ayurvedic medicine has always paid attention to these details in their healing practices, often advising people to wear their corresponding zodiacal stone as a ring or a talisman.

CRYSTALS & THE ELEMENTS

Crystals are inextricably linked to the four elements, from their original creation to their potency and use in magical rituals and healing. Formed by the combination, in varying conditions, of different physical elements, such as metals, non-metals and gases, some stones require the enormous heat generated by volcanoes or deep thermal currents to bond their molecular makeup, while others may require pressure or water sources. The effects of the four elements of Fire, Earth, Air and Water is evident in these formation processes. The heat generated by Fire, pressure from the Earth, and the chemical reactions involved in absorbing elements from the Air and Water, all demonstrate the four elements in action to produce the correct conditions and ingredients necessary for the creation of crystals, lending them each their unique qualities.

CRYSTALS & THE WATER ELEMENT

The depositing or the evaporation of Water is a component in the formation of many crystals, including stalagmites and stalactites. Water also finds its balance by assuming its appropriate state as a gas, liquid or solid (ice). Therefore, Water-inspired gemstones help to balance your emotions and influence your dreams by shifting notions between the conscious and unconscious mind.

Some Watery crystals are ★ Pearl, Beryl, Moonstone, Aquamarine, Selenite, Tourmaline and Amethyst.

THE CRYSTALLINE SYSTEM OF YOUR RULING BODY THE MOON

Associated with your ruling body the Moon, are Aquamarine, Opal, Clear Quartz, Emerald, Diamond, Selenite and of course, Moonstone. This is the fourth crystalline system, known as hexagonal, which corresponds with the Moon, being fourth on the list. The stone which perhaps represents this system best, the Emerald, or aluminium and beryllium silicate, was always regarded as having sacred qualities in ancient times. Its uses in ophthalmology, to prevent bleeding, for liver complaints, and as an antiseptic, were well-known, as was its power to stimulate the memory, which is analogous with the Moon.

THE MOON'S GEMSTONE ASSOCIATION

★ **Pearl** ★ A pearl can shine with all the silvery colours of the Moon rather than just simply white, their incandescent, shimmering colour similar to the linings of the oysters in which they are found. Pearls are linked with water and the Moon, and are symbols of spiritual wisdom, purity and hidden knowledge. As an emblem of innocence and peace, the pearl was once thought to be sacred to the Moon and the goddess of young women, Diana. In Ancient Greece, the pearl was worn by the goddess Aphrodite and their culture regarded pearls as a symbol of love, marriage and union. Aphrodite and Venus, the Roman goddess of love, were both known as 'Lady of the Pearls'. According to some traditions, pearls are said to have aphrodisiac qualities if they are worn as charms, and powdered pearls are still used in some Eastern medicine systems to produce powerful love potions. Pearls are believed to be able to wash away sins, and are also good for settling moods.

CANCER'S FEATURE CRYSTAL ★ MOONSTONE

An opalescent form of feldspar, resembling in its colour the pale lustrous gleam of moonlight, this is traditionally regarded as a stone of the Goddess and is sacred to all things Lunar and celestial. Moonstone is a translucent, milky stone which occurs in yellow, peach, grey, blue and colourless. The beautiful sheen of this stone seems to wax and wane like its namesake and the crystal has featured in much Lunar folklore, being considered a sacred link to the Moon in many cultures. Moonstone improves emotional intelligence and provides deep healing within this realm, and is believed to have the power to endow love, wealth and wisdom. Moonstone is believed to absorb the rays of the Moon, and with them some of the mystical attributes of that heavenly body. Its potency is said to increase as the Moon waxes (or goes from New to Full), and lessens when that orb declines. Moonstone is a symbol of hope and a stone of new beginnings. Like the Moon, this stone is reflective and reminds us that, as the Moon waxes and wanes, so too is everything a part of a cycle of change. Its most powerful effect is that of calming the emotions, and it is also useful in honing one's intuition and improving natural psychic abilities. It is also a stone of wishes and for working towards goal manifestation.

Moonstone can offer clarity and perspective about your place in the world, and your true path, like looking down upon your own personal world from the distance of the Moon. Possessing a gentle nature which promotes kindness and peace, it is calming, balancing, soothing, healing, protective and uplifting, particularly to those whose Moon is strong in their astrological chart. It helps to identify emotional patterns that are stored in the subconscious mind, and can act as a guardian. Moonstone opens the mind to hoping and wishing, inspiration and impulse, magic and enchantment. It grants intuitive recognition and even flashes of insight, and allows one to absorb what is needed from the Universe. Moonstone makes conscious the unconscious and promotes and enhances empathy, lucidity, clairvoyance, receptivity, serendipity and synchronicity - however, regarding these last two, care needs to be taken that it does not induce illusions in response to wishful thinking. It is helpful in times of shock, possessing a calm, flowing peace that helps restore emotional balance in everyday experiences too. Moonstone is the traditional birthstone of June, and resonates most strongly with the sign of Cancer.

CANCERIAN POWER CRYSTALS

Around six thousand years ago, in ancient Mesopotamia, the Sumerians started studying precious stones and minerals, as well as the stars, with a view of improving their lives in many ways by probing the secrets and mysteries of the Universe. Their esoteric interests and knowledge were such that they began to grasp the general connections between the Earth and the heavens, or the Solar system as they knew it, and the functions of stones and minerals as a link between the two. Their method of making these connections was by colour (for example the Sun was allocated all yellow stones), as well as other spiritual links. The gemstones listed for the portion of your zodiac sign are given their status as your 'power crystals' due to the links that can be made between your primary planetary ruler/s and your mutable planetary ruler (listed last), and each stone's particular colour, chemical and mineral compositions, healing properties, and the number they are given (based on the Mohs scale of hardness: for example, diamond scores a perfect 10 out of 10), all of which combine to align with your planetary rulers. Working mindfully with your planet's special crystals is one way you can increase the flow of power and magic into your life.

POWER CRYSTALS FOR FIRST HALF CANCERIANS ★ (21 June - 4 July)

Influenced by the Moon and Pluto

Adularia (Moonstone), Cat's Eye Scapolite, Pearl, Rose Quartz, Aragonite, Calcite, Coral

ADULARIA (MOONSTONE) ★ Probably the most precious variety of moonstone is adularia, which echoes the Moon's pearly sheen. Named after its place of discovery in Adula, Switzerland, it has a soft luminous glow. When cut in domed shapes a hovering line of light dances across its surface giving the illusion of being above the crystal, rather than coming from the fine, fibrous particles within, lending it an aura of illusion and magic.

PEARL ★ Pearls have a long, well-charted and distinguished history. Pearl is formed within bivalve mollusc shells and there are four types of this jewel - in order of value from the most expensive, they are: spherical, pear-shaped, button-shaped and irregular (baroque). Pearl is usually white, tinged with colours such as cream, yellow, pink, green, black, blue or brown. Coloured pearl is more valuable, such as the pink, bronze and black (the rarest and most expensive) varieties. Used medicinally, the pearl has been used to treat a number of physical ailments throughout history. In modern medicine, pearls that are rejected as gems are processed and ground to a fine powder, providing the pharmaceutical industry a valuable source of calcium, and the cosmetic industry an ingredient for face powders, creams and potions.

The beauty of pearls has seen them prized as a symbol of purity and love for centuries, and they can be worn to promote honesty if you wish to remain true to yourself in all that you do. Pearl can be used to attract wealth. In Indian mythology, pearl is known as the 'Mother Gem of the Sea', and is sacred to Lakshmi, the goddess of wealth. A spell to bring new fortune into one's life draws upon this legendary connection: the ritual involved throwing a small pearl that you have recently bought into a stream during the waxing Moon phase. The principle of this spell is that giving up something of value will draw more wealth into your life, and that by casting the jewel away, you have belief in your own power to attract the prosperity you desire. Pearls are also useful for releasing your past and letting go of ideas that are no longer serving you. In doing this, you are also in a better position to reassess your beliefs and current opinions, and to re-evaluate what is holding you back from achieving your true potential. Pearls are essentially a useful gemstone to work with if you are at a crossroads and needing to solidify your views with more harmonious energies in order to move forward. It is worth noting that pearls reflect and amplify the energy of the wearer, so if you are feeling down on yourself, they shouldn't be worn. However, if you are feeling positive about yourself, wearing pearls will amplify this and enhance your attractiveness, which may help draw new romance into your life, hence their well-known use as a 'love charm'. Pearls are sensitive, like their Cancerian companions, and relatively soft, with a Mohs scale hardness of only 3 to 4, and dissolve in certain conditions, so should never be immersed in any acidic liquids. They should also never be kept in a warm place, as they are made up of two per cent water and warmth may cause them to dry out or to develop cracks and fissures. For many the production and cultivation of pearls may be considered an ethical issue, for as many as 50 per cent of pearl oysters may die in the process of being suspended in ocean cages for pearl-production. If you are concerned about the moral side of pearl farming, it would be wise to know where you are sourcing your gems from, and their ethical standards and practices. Despite its fragile physical nature, the pearl's legendary beauty endures. Diamond has been known for centuries as the king of gems, due to its stunning sparkle and almost invincible structure; but the pearl is rightly considered the queen, for its pure beauty.

ROSE QUARTZ ★ This soft pink translucent stone is quite simply and universally known as the 'love stone'. Unobtrusive though it is, this stone should never be underrated. The minuscule crystals of which it is composed give it amazing durability, and the addition of titanium, a metallic element of profound strength, not only accounts for its agreeable colouring but gives it the power to work wonders on physical and emotional pains and scars. Calming to the spirit and banishing fear and violent tendencies, aggressive energies find it difficult to survive in its presence. It is connected with the Heart chakra and is the stone of unconditional love, enhancing all forms of love and opening up the heart. It is excellent for increasing self-worth and acceptance. Its pink colour associated with Venus, the planet of love and desire, rose quartz is tender and passionate, erotic and nurturing, affectionate and amorous, all at the same time. Like Venus, this crystal's energies also promote receptivity to beauty of all kinds. Reassuring and soft, it helps to strengthen your empathy and sensitivity. If you have never received love, it will fill your heart; if you have loved and lost, it comforts your grief. Balancing and calming, rose quartz has been used for centuries to heal the heart, attract love, ease emotional pain, foster self-acceptance, treat fertility problems, overcome traumas, and develop a spirit of forgiveness and trust. It is a gentle stone, helping to balance all of the bodily systems and restoring a sensitive of peace and tranquillity; it is an excellent stone to use for bringing harmony to a chaotic situation. It can be placed under the pillow to encourage more restful sleep and ease insomnia. Useful during stressful, dramatic or traumatic situations, rose quartz can empower you to feel more positive, potent, loving and accepting. Holding, wearing or carrying it also enhances positive affirmations. However, because this stone absorbs negative energies, it should be cleansed regularly if used for healing purposes. It can be cleaned under fresh, running water, then left out in the Sun for a short period to dry. The energies this soothing stone radiates can and should be shared, by giving rose quartz to those in need of comfort a boost of self-confidence and reassurance. Overall, rose quartz has the power to instil infinite peace into your heart. Releasing emotional wounds, encouraging forgiveness and compassion of the self and others, and assisting with all matters of love, it heals and opens your heart on every level, teaching the true essence of love.

CALCITE ★ Calcite, a translucent, waxy, often banded gemstone, comes in over 700 varieties and a vast array of colours, such as green, yellow, blue, orange, brown, pink, grey, red and clear. In crystal therapy it is a powerful amplifier and cleanser of energy. Calcite has been used for thousands of years for healing purposes, and each colour corresponds with unique healing properties and different chakras within the body. However, most calcites regardless of colour, share some similar characteristics. Simply having this stone in the room cleans negative energies from the environment and enhances your own energy, and within the body it removes stagnant energy. Aiding in becoming more energetic on all levels, it combats laziness, encourages motivation, and has an overall positive, uplifting effect. Calcite is an active crystal, speeding up development and growth, and is also a spiritual stone linked to the higher consciousness. It accelerates spiritual development and helps create emotional intelligence by connecting the emotions to the intellect. Calcite facilitates the opening up of psychic abilities, channelling, and astral experience. Mentally, it calms the mind, teaches discernment and analysis, boosts memory and stimulates insights, making it a useful stone for study. Emotionally, calcite alleviates emotional stress and restores serenity. A stabilising stone, it enhances group cooperation by transmuting negative energies and calling in higher forces to facilitate harmony between people.

CORAL ★ Coral is among the most ancient of gem materials and was first used for adornment in prehistoric times. The name comes from a Greek word that means 'nymph of the sea'. Long regarded as a powerful talisman that was able to stop bleeding, give protection from evil spirits and even ward off hurricanes, red coral is renowned for its strength and energy. The wearing of coral was reputed to cure or prevent many ailments, and as an amulet it banished nightmares, protected children and warded off demons of the darkness, so in this sense it could be used as a protective gem. The coral used in jewellery is the hard skeleton formed by certain polyps of the corallium nobile family and occurs in red, blue, golden, black, white and pink. These polyps are minute living creatures that live in vast colonies. When they die, their skeletal remains - mostly calcium carbonate - build up to form massive coral reefs. Red coral is considered the best colour for protective charms and is called 'Witch Stone' in Italy. It was thought to absorb emotional negativity and was used against the Evil Eye. Coral, particularly red coral, encourages one to have more determination and courage. As an ocean dweller, coral's astrological correspondence is with the Moon, which also befits its watery genesis. When sourcing your coral, however, you should bear in mind that coral reefs are among the world's most vital yet fragile ecosystems and materials taken from them should only be purchased from a sustainable marine operator.

POWER CRYSTALS FOR SECOND HALF CANCERIANS ★ (5 - 21 July)

Influenced by the Moon and Neptune
Water Opal, Coral *, Desert Rose, Selenite, Water Nodule (Enhydrous)

CORAL ★ Please see under previous subtitle: *'Power Crystals for First Half Cancerians'*

OPAL ★ This is a beautiful and delicate stone with a fine vibration, reminding us of the wondrous unfolding of the Divine Universe. As it contains all the colours of the other stones, it can be used to amplify all other stones' energies. Unlike most other gemstones, opal is not crystalline in form, but rather is defined as a mineraloid. It is an amorphous silica variety of quartz, is comparatively soft, and owes its beauty to the wonderful play of colour from its surface. The mineral is formed from the shells or skeletons of very tiny plant and animal organisms, and occurs in many different colours and varieties, such as fire opal, girasol quartz, moss opal, milk opal, precious opal and resin opal, among others. Bringing miraculous order to a vast array of patterns and colours, the opal unites heaven and Earth in a union of water and fire. The characteristically iridescent, rainbow hues of the gem are caused by irregular refraction of light from its surface, which is traversed by innumerable tiny cracks. In the process of its formation, the surface becomes covered by these cracks, and these crevices become filled in with a substance containing more or less water than the surrounding surface. A great irregularity and refraction and a play of colour varies according to the angle from which the gem is viewed: blue, perhaps when looked at in one direction, yellow or crimson if we view it from another. Known as the Queen of Gems, opal is one of the most beautiful stones and has been highly prized for thousands of years. Opals have always generated strong passions, according to the folklore of many cultures. In Ancient Egypt and Babylon, opals were considered a powerful healing gem, combining the qualities of fire and water, and were said to bring good luck. Opal was also sacred to medieval England, Greece and some Arabic societies. Opal is said to improve vitality by magnifying energy, enhance one's self-image, improve one's fortune or luck, have protective powers, stimulate cosmic consciousness and induce psychic visions. It is considered capable of opening up the Third Eye and Crown chakras, and above other minerals is used by many mystics to lead them into supernatural and otherworldly realms. Absorbent and reflective, on a spiritual level opal picks up thoughts and feelings, amplifies them, and returns them to Source. A protective and karmic stone, it teaches that what you put out comes back. An excellent aid for transformation, opal enhances self-worth and helps you understand your full potential. It stimulates originality and dynamic creativity, and encourages an interest in the arts. Opal is also associated with desire and eroticism, love and passion; it is a seductive stone that intensifies emotional states and dissolves inhibitions. It can also help you gain access to your true self, magnifying your personality traits and bringing them to the surface for healing. Overall, opal will work well with the emotional, mental, spiritual and etheric bodies. It can provide a much-needed burst of energy, boost self-confidence, enhance creativity and intuition, help release anger, and connect one to the Higher Self. Opal contains more water than any other mineral, up to 21 per cent, and is porous, so it should not be immersed in water or brought into contact with oils, as these may harm or destroy it.

SELENITE ★ Selenite is a form of gypsum that is called selenite if it is relatively clear and well-formed. It has a hardness of 2, and some selenite crystals have the startling property of being soft and flexible enough to be bent in one's hands. This crystal can be colourless (similar to clear quartz in appearance), white, green, grey or golden-brown, and is found in many countries including Australia, Greece, and the Americas, and the ones from Mexico are the most popular ones for metaphysical use, being used to make spheres, lamps, wands and a variety of other spiritual tools and talismans. Its keywords are spiritual activation, communion with the 'higher self', attuning one to the Universal mind, and the integration of heart awareness with the brain and mind. Selenite quickly opens and activates the Third Eye, Crown and Soul Star (above the head) Chakras. In fact, its intensity is quite remarkable, and a wand made from this crystal pointed at the Third Eye sends energy that can feel like a gust of wind going through the forehead and out the top of the head; attaching other stones to a selenite wand can also magnify those stones' energies. Fast and effective at cleansing one's auric field, it can raise one's awareness to higher planes of inner experience as well, making it possible to meet one's spirit guides and guardian angels. In meditation, selenite stimulates the flow of spiritual energies throughout one's physical body, as well as the astral and etheric bodies. Selenite, especially the clear selenite variety that occurs in wand form, is deeply linked with the Water element; in fact, Water occurs in the interior of many of these wands, and water is key in the growth of selenite. The huge selenite crystals from Chihuahua, Mexico, were formed in a water-saturated cave. Selenite, when used in meditation, can assist in facilitating the integration of the left and right sides of the brain. The great 'myth' of the human condition portrays these two brains as if they were separate beings - the rational/materialist left and the idealist/creative right. The resolution of their seemingly insoluble conflict can instigate great healing, particularly within the Watery second-half Cancerian's soul, for whom this is a power crystal.

YOUR LUCKY NUMBERS

Your lucky numbers are ★ 8 for Cancer ^ & 2 for the Moon (also, see 'Lucky Magic Square of the Moon')

LUCKY MAGIC SQUARE OF THE MOON

In Western occult tradition, each planet has traditionally been associated with a series of numbers and particular arrangements of those numbers. One such method of numerological organisation is the magic square. Magic squares date back to ancient times, appearing in China about 3,000 years ago. The first Chinese square is seen in the scroll of the river Lo - the Lo-Shu, a scroll believed to have been created by Fuh-Hi, the mythical founder of Chinese civilisation. Certain squares came to be linked with the planets; these associations came from the Babylonians. Each *kamea*, or magic square, is linked with a particular planet, and each of the squares has a *seal*, which is the geometric pattern created by following the numbers in order of their value. This pattern touches upon all the numbers of the square and the seal is used to represent the entire square. An intelligence and a spirit are also associated with each kamea, derived from the key numbers contained within it, using a Hebrew form of numerology. This intelligence is viewed as an inspiring, guiding and informing entity.

The 'Magic Square of the Moon ' is divided into 81 cells, or squares, nine across and nine down. The sum of the numbers in the vertical, horizontal and diagonal lines is a constant of 369. The total of these numbers is 3321. Therefore, the numbers 9, 81, 369 and 3321 are also assigned to the Moon.

YOUR NUMEROLOGY NUMBER & LUCKY SUN SIGN NUMBERS

"Everything that exists has a vibration. The vibration of sound, music, colour, matter, even our words, thoughts, and names show form. All vibration is measurable. To measure we need numbers. Numbers are the basis of all. Numbers are the key to all mysteries."
Shirley Blackwell Lawrence, *Behind Numerology*

Numerology is essentially the metaphysical * 'science' of numbers. The use of numbers in magic is its cornerstone of power. The ancient Greek philosopher and mathematician Pythagoras, born around 590 BC, embarked on a thirty-year spiritual quest studying with important religious and esoteric teachers and healers to find the mystery of 'The Hidden Light', and came to see mankind as living in three worlds: the natural, the human and the Divine. He asserted that all things can be expressed in numerical terms, because they are ultimately reducible to numbers. Pythagoras stated that "Numbers are the first things of all of Nature" and followed the theory that "Nothing can exist without numbers."

Many believe that numbers have an arcane, mystical relationship with words, and with inanimate and animate objects; the interpretations that arose from these relationships date back to a time when the dawning intelligence of primitive man first visualised the meaning of numbers and associated it with spiritual significance. Numerology is the science of the exploration of this relationship in order to discover hidden meanings, forecast the future or interpret the character of a person. In its more modern applications, a series of figures which correspond to an individual's name and date of birth are calculated, and practitioners believe one's prospects, fortune and character can be deciphered from the results ^.

So what is numerology and how does one use it? Everything in the Universe has a vibrational frequency, an energy, a force, all vibrating at various rates, and we as humans are no exception, the difference between one person and another is their rate of vibration. This force or energy is constantly in motion and changing, and we can even 'tune into' and feel our vibrations if we are still for long enough.

Along with letters, sounds, colours, crystals, and many other things, it is believed that numbers also have vibrations, and when we are able to familiarise ourselves with our own numerical frequencies, we can use this familiarity to add power and magic to our lives. The numbers of our birth date, the letters of our names, and the numbers of our Sun sign and ruling planets, all have a unique vibrational frequency, and herein lies the key to understanding our self and our journey through life. Numerology refers to the knowledge contained within the numbers of our birth date and our name, and this is our own personal magic which can greatly assist us through life.

* Metaphysics is the study of those sciences that extend beyond the physical or tangible

HOW TO FIND YOUR NUMEROLOGY NUMBER

^ Your Sun sign's number was added up according to the principle of corresponding a number with a letter, for example 1=A, 2=B, 3=C and so on in sequence and up to 9=I, then beginning again at number 1 for the next letter J and following this same sequence. Following this system, the sum of the letters in Cancer vibrate to the number 8.

Your personal numerology number is determined by adding up all the numbers in your birth date until they reach a two-digit figure. The two resulting numbers are then added together again to form a single digit, which is your personal numerology number. For example, someone born on 3 February 1983, would add the digits $3 + 2 + 1 + 9 + 8 + 3 = 26 =$ (reduced to two digits) 8. So that person's personal numerology birth number is 8.

Each primary number or birth number from 1 to 9 has a specific meaning and is governed by a planetary force. The principle of numerology reduces all numbers down to the following: 1 to 9, and 10, 11, 13 and 22 *. The last four numbers only apply to people specially concerned with the occult and spiritualism - and can be studied at greater length through other sources if so desired - and can in any case be reduced further to a single digit if preferred. Your birth number contains a unique power, and therein lie your strengths, shortcomings and opportunities. It is beyond the scope of this book to outline your individual numerology number possibilities, so for the purposes of astrological applications, I have only included your Sun sign and ruling planet's special numbers.

* The numbers 10 and 13, and the master numbers 11 and 22, can be further reduced to one digit if so desired; however, they can be interpreted as they are without further reduction. The choice is personal.

BASIC MEANINGS & KEYWORDS

1 ★ Sun. Masculine influence, beginnings, independence, inventiveness, originality, leadership, exploration, innovation, ambition.
2 ★ Moon. Feminine influence, cooperation, partnership, tact, diplomacy, harmony, unity, emotions, imagination, adaptability.
3 ★ Jupiter. Communication, expression, youthfulness, self-confidence, creativity, inspiration, optimism, curiosity.
4 ★ Uranus. Order, form, security, stability, patience, restriction, work, values, practicality.
5 ★ Mercury. Freedom, inconsistency, change, variety, travel, activity, learned.
6 ★ Venus. Love, home, family, sense of duty, responsibility, marriage, justice, nurturing, balance, gentleness, peace, friendship.
7 ★ Neptune. Analysis, wisdom, mystical, spiritual, solitude, precision, research, integrity, mystery, psychic perceptions.

8 ★ Saturn. Money, power, success, organisation, hard work, business, health, purpose, control, authority, mastery.

9 ★ Mars. Completion, endings, Universal, service, humanity, philanthropy, loyalty.

10 ★ Fortunate, creative, vibrant, stable, optimistic, original, successful, determined, individualistic.

11 ★ Master number. Prophecies, inspiration, moral courage, missionary, long-suffering, foolhardiness, enlightenment, invention.

13 ★ Misunderstood, fearful, changeable, interested in the occult, fatalistic, flexible, sacred, beguiling.

22 ★ Master number. Powerful, successful, idealistic, attracted to the occult, creative, wise, successful, masterful, spiritually understanding.

★ THE NUMBER 2 - FOR THE MOON ★

Names ★ Duo, Duality, Double, Binary, Duad

Arithmomantic connections with the letters of the alphabet ★ B, K and T

Ruled by the Moon, the planet which fosters harmony by favouring love, union, cooperation, compromise, passivity, diplomacy, tact, negotiation, settlements, and all mutually beneficial ventures, 2 is a gentle, considerate and sensitive vibration. The number 2 is the mediator and peace-maker, representing the first divergence from the unity represented by the number 1. As such, it signifies the first opportunity for diversity and conflict. On the other hand, it represents the first flowering of the creative principle, and is a symbol of fertility, for male and female, positive and negative, spirit and matter, and also for that part of ourselves that enables us to turn and look at ourselves, allowing for self-reflection and therefore, greater conscious awareness of self. Duality, the number 2, or the Duad as it was called by Pythagoreans, represents both diversity and equality or justice. This idea of diversity originates from the idea of two opposites, such as good and evil, night and day, joy and pain, love and hate, riches and poverty. Yet, at the same time, both sides of a question must be always heard, so the number 2 also stands for concord, harmony, response, balance and sympathy. Arguably one of the most beautiful symbols representing the perfect unity formed by the number 2, is that of yin and yang, as depicted in the Tao in China. When early humankind became aware of the binary rhythms upon which the great symphony of nature is based, and which is at the heart of nature itself, it became aware of everything which is double: sky and Earth, male and female, hot and cold, day and night, high and low, life and death, Sun and Moon, inside and outside, pure and impure, good and evil. Carrying the vibes of the Moon, it stands for social enjoyment, cooperation and companionship. Since it soothes an aggressive spirit, it is suited to those who like a gentle, congenial way of life, those who wish for nurturing, intimate partnerships, and who love to pass their time daydreaming. Number 2s are prone to being real softies. Warm-hearted, trustworthy and diplomatic to the utmost, they love any form of art and craft, especially music. While number 2 people are placid and show great consideration for the feelings of others, you may be spoiled, over-dependent, passive-aggressive, manipulative, lazy and careless. You are very easy to make friends with, and usually become a great success socially because of your ability to sympathise with all types of character. In fact, there are no actively adverse influences of this number; your faults are mostly passive ones. However, your dislike of discord and strife may create a shirking of all worry and difficulties, and a refusal to shoulder responsibility. You are gentle, sensitive, cooperative, tactful, a peacemaker, studious, loving, patient, musical, feminine, harmonious, passive, artistic, sensual and intuitive. Number 2 individuals are more geared to thought than to action, and although you are inventive, you will be less forceful in carrying out your plans. You are likely to possess charm and intuitive powers, but you may suffer from a lack of self-confidence. You are changeable, perhaps even deceitful, and may be over-sensitive and depressive. You tend to get on well with your opposites, Number 1 people. Overall, number 2 is a feminine number and Monday is your special day.

Alchemy ★ This number represents two forces opposing *or* complementing one another. It often stands for male and female, positive and negative, light and dark, and heaven and Earth. In spiritual teaching, it can be used to represent the division between God and man, sometimes known as the 'Lover and the Beloved'. In alchemy, a separation from one into two is essential to release the vital energy that a polarity generates.

LUCKY 'MAGIC HOURS' OR 'TIME UNITS'

One rule of magic, luck and power, as already outlined elsewhere in this book, can be found within the well-known phrase, "As above, so below." From the most ancient times, the planets were said to rule Earthly destinies and powers. Days of the week were named after the seven planets which were the only ones then known: Sun Day, Moon Day, Mars Day (French: Mardi), Mercury Day (French: Mercredi), Jove Day (French: Jeudi), Venus Day (French: Vendredi) and Saturn Day.

The planetary hours are based on an ancient astrological system, the Chaldean order of the planets. The Chaldean order indicates the relative orbital velocity of the planets, and from a heliocentric (helios = The Sun) perspective, this sequence also indicates the relative distance of the planets from the Sun (the Sun switching places with the Earth in this sequence), and the distance of the Moon from the Earth.

Before an action is taken in daily life, or a transaction undertaken, for instance, it is possible to choose the appropriate day and hour that will provide the greatest chances of success. By studying the planetary hours system, you will discover which actions are propitious to which of the seven planets or 'star-gods' and at what time it would be advisable to undertake them.

The planetary hours system uses this Chaldean order to divide time, and each planetary hour of the planetary day is ruled by a different planet. The order is repeated, starting with the slowest: Saturn - then, Jupiter, Mars, Sun, Venus, Mercury, Moon, then back to Saturn, Jupiter, Mars, etc, ad infinitum. The planet that rules the first hour of the day is also the ruler of that whole day and gives the day its name. So the first hour of Saturday is ruled by Saturn, the first hour of Sunday by the Sun, and so on. It is important, for the purposes of using specific planetary energies for our magic and wishes, to note that planetary hours are not considered the same length as our normal time-keeping slots of sixty minutes. Each day is split into time periods, day time and night time, beginning at around sunrise and sunset respectively. These two time periods are each divided into twelve equal-length hours, which are the planetary hours. So the planetary hours of the day and the planetary hours of the night will be of different lengths, except during the equinoxes when light and darkness are balanced.

In sequence, the Sun, Moon and the five visible planets each exerts its own special influence over a twenty-four-hour period. I like to call your planet's special day and hour the 'Magic Hour'.

Magic rituals to draw luck and love to you should be conducted at astrologically correct times and with the appropriate instruments, tools, cards, herbs, flowers, oils and plants which are linked with the ruling planet. For example, a love ritual, spell or potion demands a concoction of any or all of the above ruled by Venus. Do not underestimate rulerships, for they wield an unseen power that can help make our dreams, big and small, come true.

Further, as specific hours of each day are ruled by certain planets, if you are really serious about attracting some power, luck or magic into your life, it is imperative that you wish, pray or ask at the most opportune times for your Sun sign. There are two methods you can use for fine tuning your magical workings. The first method is to perform your spell, ritual or wishing on the day your Sun sign's ruling planet during the planetary hour that signifies the essence of what you are asking for (e.g. A Cancerian who is looking for love might perform a love-seeking ritual on a Monday, during a Venus-ruled planetary hour). Alternatively, if you wish to summon the power of your Sun sign's own ruling planet, then that same Cancerian might perform their love-seeking ritual on a Friday (ruled by Venus) during the Moon's planetary hour.

The nature of that which you are asking for, such as love, travel opportunities, money, career guidance, protection or friendship for example, should always be considered when choosing the day or hour during which your magic will be heightened.

The answer to the question why are there seven days in a week, is a very important one to know in unravelling the secret of your Magic Hours. Ancient people recognised the supreme importance of the seven heavenly spheres, which comprised those which could be seen by the naked eye: the Sun, Moon, Mercury, Venus, Mars, Jupiter and Saturn. They then named each of the seven days of the week after one of those spheres and assigned that planetary 'ruler' to one day of the week. As viewed from Earth, these seven spheres appear to move at varying speeds, and the ancients used this factor to arrange them in order of varying speed. If you intend to use your Magic Hours to attract wonderful things, you must memorise that sequence because it is what forms the basis of the whole system.

Whenever you intend to use your Magic Hours or, perhaps more accurately, Magic *Time Units*, it is important to find out the exact time of sunrise for the area in which you live, as sunrise marks the time when your planet's magic is at its most powerful on its specific day. So, at sunrise on Sunday, the Sun rules the hour following the sunrise, the Moon rules the first hour following sunrise on a Monday, and through the week the pattern is repeated, with each day's ruling planet beginning the cycle in that first hour after dawn. It is logical then, that the rest of the planets, in sequence, follow on with one planet per hour for that day thereafter for the rest of the 24 hour cycle, creating a Magic Hour or Time Unit for each planet throughout the day and night, depending on which planet rules that particular day and is therefore the first in line.

If you wish to explore the idea in more depth, it is worth noting first and foremost that each day contains twenty-four hours, but, depending on the season, day and night will be of varying lengths. In summer, daylight is longer than darkness, whereas the reverse applies in winter. During autumn and spring, day and night are usually about equal. Therefore, although a complete day always contains twenty-four hours, there are not always twelve hours between sunrise and sunset and another twelve hours between sundown and the following sunrise. So, depending on the season (and location), a time unit may be shorter than one hour, longer than one hour, or equal to one hour. So whenever you intend to use your Magic Time Units, it is important to find out the exact time of sunrise and sunset for the area in which you live. The next step is to divide the amount of day time (if day when you wish to work your 'magic', otherwise the same following theory applies to night time) into twelve equal sections by calculating the number of hours and minutes between sunrise and sunset and divide by twelve. An example is if the Sun rises at 6.27 a.m. and sets at 5.49 p.m., the amount of time contained in this day is eleven hours and twenty-two minutes. Convert this total into minutes (682) and then divide that figure by twelve (57). Therefore, each of the twelve daylight time units will be 57 minutes on that day.

Although this wonderful method of using astrology is very ancient, it may be completely new to you. You are in for a pleasant surprise though, because if you are willing to delve into a little research and put the system to the test, rich rewards are in store for you!

YOUR LUCKY DAY ★ MONDAY

Planet ★ The Moon
Basic Energy ★ Protection, Psychism, Wishes
Element ★ Water
Colours ★ White, Silver or Blue

Energy Keywords ★ Creativity, Intuition, Mothering, Feeling, Kindness, Protection, Domesticity, Flexibility, Sympathy, Growth, Imagination, Impressionism, Magnetism, Peace, Plasticity, Sensitivity, Psychism, Receptivity, Vision, & Cycles

Monday is the day of the Moon, your ruler. In commonly used calendars, Monday is the second day of the week, though in others it is the first. The English name is derived from Old English *Monandaeg*, and Middle English *Monenday*, meaning 'Moon Day'. A number of songs feature Monday, often lyrically associating it with melancholy, depression or anxiety.

In the folk rhyme 'Monday's Child', 'Monday's child is fair of face'. Monday is for Moon Magic. Her silvery light can be used to strengthen psychic, intuitive, imaginative or dreaming powers, to enhance your ability to meditate or to be inspired by your inner depths. There are many Moon goddesses if you are requiring extra help, and even the Egyptian god Thoth is a ruler of Lunar power.

THE MOON'S MAGIC TIME UNITS
(BASED ON THE PLANETARY HOURS)
FOR EACH DAY OF THE WEEK

SATURDAY ★ Seventh time unit after sunrise
SUNDAY ★ Fourth and Eleventh time units after sunrise
MONDAY ★ First and Eighth time units after sunrise
TUESDAY ★ Fifth and Twelfth time units after sunrise
WEDNESDAY ★ Second and Ninth time units after sunrise
THURSDAY ★ Sixth time unit after sunrise
FRIDAY ★ Third and Tenth time units after sunrise **

Choose the Hour/s of the Moon for any transaction, initiative, exchange, activity or venture which is likely to involve your family, your mother, children, domestic tending, love, nurturing, home comforts, security, privacy, tenacity, sending emotional messages, psychicism, Lunar magic, visionary work, water divination, and anything else to do with cycles, things of a fluctuating nature (such as the stock exchange), rhythms and water.

** Please note that for the purposes of simplification, the information regarding 'The Moon's Magic Time Units' is a very diluted and simplified version of using magical times to your advantage. These hours cover only daylight hours, or the first twelve hours after sunrise, and do not take into account magical times after sunset or throughout the night. 'Hours' is also a deceptive term, as most 'time periods' used in this system are less than an hour, but for the purposes of simplifying the technique, I refer to them as Magic Hours (to keep with the tradition of the term 'planetary hours') rather than magic 'time units', which is what they really are. Should you wish to do further research on your ruling planet's most powerful time units, or require further information about the planet/s from which you are seeking 'energy' from in order to assist your wish-making, other sources may provide you with more comprehensive and detailed information.

A LITTLE NEW MOON / MAGICAL TIME UNIT WISH RITUAL

Step 1 ~ Choose the Magical Hour and/or day that matches your intentions. The first dawn hour of Sunday, ruled by the Sun, is a great time for all-purpose magic, success, joy, abundance, prosperity, bliss, personal power & all-round expansion.

Step 2 ~ Write out a little wish list with the appropriate coloured pen on the colour paper which corresponds to your desire.

Step 3 ~ Choose a small stone of your choosing that is connected to your wish (or a number of stones that are perhaps linked with your planetary ruler's number, for example 2 for the Moon).

Step 4 ~ Find a nice patch of soil in your garden or any special place to you, dig into it, affirm your wish in your mind, place the crystal/s and piece of paper in the hole, then place a plant on top of the crystal/s and wish list.

Step 5 ~ Fill the soil back in over the roots of the plant and feed it with a little water out of a magical vessel (a small genie bottle would be ideal).

Step 6 ~ Thank the Earth, the Universe and the Sun (or whatever planet you are summoning the power from) for bringing forth your desires.

Step 7 ~ Repeat all day long: "Thank You, Thank You, Thank You!"

Step 8 ~ Watch your plant - and your wish - grow bigger and bigger as time goes on!

YOUR LUCKY CHARM/TALISMANS

The following are three 'materials' or talismanic symbols from which to make your lucky charms, and the planetary energy under which to do it, corresponding with your Sun sign:

CANCER ★ Ruby, Anchor, Silver, the Moon

"When any star ascends fortunately, take a stone and herb that are under that star, make a ring of the metal that is congruous therewith, and in that fix the stone with the herb under it."
Henry Cornelius Agrippa, *On Occult Philosophy*

Charms, talismans and amulets are among the oldest forms of magic. A charm or talisman is a symbol, often used to communicate a thought, prayer or wish to, or to make a connection with the Divine. It is usually in the form of an object, which has been imbued with mysterious and magical powers. A charm may be as simple as a stone, a flower or a feather, or it might be a parchment bearing writing; the meaning and significance that you attribute to the symbol is what is important. It can be created by yourself (to best effect) or by someone else, and works as a tool to activate our subconscious mind.

You can use general charms such as a cross, or a universally lucky symbol such as a horseshoe, but you will exude and therefore attract more potency and protection if you make and wear the appropriate charms with the matching gemstone, set in the right metal and created under the corresponding planetary influence. While most people wear silver or gold, cheaper tin or copper may be more appropriate and indeed beneficial for your Sun sign. An amulet (for protection) or a talisman or charm (for luck), must also be made, ordered, designed or purchased on the appropriate day of the week for its power to be most effective. Your day, as previously described, is Monday.

You can even go further and create or buy your amulet or charm at one of the hours and/or days when your planet is exerting its most powerful influence. It may sound complicated and requiring of forethought and effort, but if you are going to summon magic and are superstitious enough to truly *believe* that you can do this (and remember pure belief in something is the starting point of all manifestation), you should be scrupulous enough to do it properly. For your planet's day and time, please consult the information under the previous headings 'Your Lucky Day' and 'The Moon's Magic Time Units'.

GODS, GODDESSES, ANIMAL TOTEMS & OTHER 'GUIDES'

Gods, goddesses and guides can be summoned to help you live your life to its optimal best. Some are connected with your Sun sign, while others may be of your own personal choosing, ones you may feel particularly drawn towards. Those which align with your ruling planet and your Sun sign, give a good indication of those who will shine a guiding light along your desired path, but you can choose your own too, based upon exploration, observations, research, meditation or simple intuition - I believe choosing your own, based on your inner *knowing* or guidance system, is a very powerful magical tool. However, to get you started, following are some animal spirit guide ideas for your contemplation. Good luck!

YOUR LUCKY ANIMALS & BIRDS

Crab, Otter, Seal, Eel, Seagull, Frog, Shellfish, Water-dwelling Birds, Stag, Heifer, Moth, Unicorn, White Peacock, Owl, Woodpecker

"Somewhere beyond the walls of our awareness … the wilderness side, the hunter side, the seeking side of ourselves is waiting to return."
Laurens van der Post, *The Heart of the Hunter*

"(People) everywhere are being made acutely aware of the fact that something essentially to life and wellbeing is flickering very low in the human species and threatening to go out entirely. This 'something' has to do with such values as love, unselfishness, sincerity, loyalty to one's best friend, honesty, enthusiasm, humility, goodness, happiness … fun. Practically every animal has these assets in abundance and is eager to share them, given the opportunity and the encouragement."
Jay Allen Boone, *Kinship with All Life*

Some astrological systems, such as Shamanistic * or Native American Astrology, tell us that the Sun sign we were born under has a corresponding animal totem, which informs us about our characteristics and act as a kind of spiritual guide or mentor throughout our life's journey. These totems are described as Solar totems, because many of them share similarities with the Solar system and the sign the Sun was passing through at the time of our birth, and therefore relate to animals and animal behaviours which also correspond to environmental conditions and seasonal changes. These animals encompass many aspects of the Solar system, from seasonal relationships, to creature instincts, to reciprocal links with the planetary vibrations, and 'clans' within nature that you are inherently closely connected with through your date of birth.

Carl Jung, a master of dream analysis and interpretation, proposed that animals symbolise our natural instincts, operating through our dreams. He theorised that certain dream symbols, among them animals, represent core emotions and concepts, archetypes that will hold true for all of us the world over, regardless of so-called 'divisions' such as sex, customs, age or culture. In *Man and His Symbols*, Jung states that primitive societies believed that each person had a bush soul and a human soul. The bush soul incarnates as a tree or animal - a totem - and when the bush soul is harmed or injured, the human soul is considered injured as well.

Some of the most important and powerful spirit guides are those belonging to the animal kingdom. Both in ancient times and in some traditional modern tribal systems, people consult with animals for their wisdom and personal power. Even though most societies today have drifted away from this connection, it has never really left us, and different creatures continue to communicate with us on both the physical and spiritual planes in an attempt to speak to our souls and spirits.

As part of the teaching world, animals can bring us wisdom and survival skills, while others show us how to adapt, transcend or morph. Others still can remind us the importance of play and humour, and guide us around how to overcome life's challenges. Many are known for their loyalty and ability to love unconditionally and without judgement, while some have a grounded and healthy detachment, remaining true to themselves rather than pleasing others, an important lesson in itself. Whatever the qualities of the unique animal guides for your Sun sign, all have some enlightening soul-awakening traits that can teach us much about our own true inner selves. Ultimately, your animal spirit guides, and in particular your Solar totem animal, endow you with qualities that will enhance your life and help to activate your creativity, wisdom and intuition, helping to heal the broken or return the lost pieces of your soul and reconnect you to the natural world.

Your Solar totem animal (listed last on your lucky birds and animals list) is not the same as an animal spirit guide, which is based on metaphysical principles and is also based on your soul's mission in this embodiment - however, you can definitely make your birth Solar totem animal your spiritual guide if you wish, as you may find that its qualities, traits, symbolism and messages strongly reflect and define your own nature - or what you aspire to become, manifest or draw towards you. Your birth totem power animal comes from a place of trust and innocence, and represents the essence of your creative inner child. If you spend some time meditating on your Solar totem animal, asking what lessons it can teach, and reflect deeply on its character, life and habits, you may find it connects with you on a deep spiritual level and you can make the necessary changes to your life to draw in more magic and power.

Overall, if your life is stagnant or in need of healing or an energy boost, you can request your animal spirit or spirits to come and help you change your vibration, awaken your truth and arouse your inner forces. If you are aware of your animal spirit's presence in your life every day, you can use its particular energies to support, guide and teach you. And above all, pay attention to any signs and expressions of its lessons, and remember to thank your chosen animal guide for helping you.

* Shamanism is a traditional spiritual practice of the Native American culture. A shaman, one who practices this age-old art, is an intermediary between the human world and the world of the spirits. He inherits his magical powers at birth, but spends many years as an apprentice, so that he is usually much older in age before he is able to practice and call upon his skills. People ask for a shaman's help when there is a crisis on either a personal or wider spread scale, such as famine, drought, war or illness. The shaman makes contact with the spirits by going into a trance. First, he may perform a series of rituals, which usually include drumming, singing and chanting, and when these have brought on the right conditions, he leaves his body behind to travel to the other world. There he meets with the spirits of his ancestors, who inform him what must be done to relieve the suffering of his people. If the shaman is asked to cure someone of a dis-ease, then the spirits may accompany him to find the correct medicinal herbs or treatments for his patient.

YOUR FEATURE ANIMAL ★ WOODPECKER

The Woodpecker's Message ★ When opportunity knocks, answer the door
Brings the totem gift of ★ Loyalty, protection, resourcefulness, discernment
Shares the power energies of ★ Progress, support, nurturance
Brings forth and teaches the magic of ★ Listening, sympathy and devotion

The Woodpecker is a little worker who brings us closer to the healing energies of Mother Earth and teaches us to protect our environment - before it is too late. The Woodpecker also represents knowledge of personal truth, mental fortitude and inner strength. Known as the Earth's drummer, this little bird is connected with Native American drumming; drumming is the heartbeat of Mother Earth and is associated with shamanism and the ability to move into other dimensions at will. The Woodpecker represents self-discovery for those born with this totem, for as you peck into trees you uncover hidden layers of the psyche. Those with this medicine make excellent analysts and possess strong mental capabilities, enabling them to delve into the minds of others, and their own minds, with accuracy and an intuitive sensitivity. The flight patterns of Woodpeckers are unique, and those with this totem will often find that their life's path won't always conform to society's standards, and that their own personal and unique rhythms need to be honoured and nurtured. Woodpeckers teach us to honour our personal truths and move through life with inner strength and perseverance. By staying grounded and maintaining our rhythms, our goals will be more easily attained.

Symbolically, Woodpeckers can represent opportunity, and reminds us of the old adage, "When opportunity knocks, answer the door." Driven, determined and persevering, the Woodpecker is extremely opportunistic, and each tree to them is a door, revealing tender morsels of food, treats and rewards, while other trees may provide shelter for their young.

The symbolic meaning of Woodpeckers can also point to a need for creative vision and capitalising on available resources; being opportunistic, the Woodpecker can see potential and value in everything, including dead trees.

The Woodpecker also reminds us to be mindful of our words, and to be succinct in our use of them. This symbolism stems from the fact that the Woodpecker has a narrow tongue, which is extremely effectively in getting to food in tight places, and therefore teaches that we should use the narrowest (and most efficient) route to make the most profound impact. In this way, it invites us to use fewer words for a stronger effect.

Further the Woodpecker indicates a return to our roots, and a need to trust our basic instincts. Dr. Carl Jung observed this bird as a symbol of the return to the 'womb' of creativity. This symbolism may be trying to tell you that you need to breathe new life into a project, through building your home even in an old, withering tree, for even in an apparently infertile place we can bring it to life through our imagination - and build our very own castle within. The Woodpecker's home in the tree is analogous of a fierce determination to return to and protect that which is sacred to us. As your power animal, this bird is calling you to return to your roots, back to the womb in which you gave birth to your ideas.

Native American wisdom also acknowledged the home-based protective themes around the Woodpecker, and gave it the title of 'protector of humankind', due to its ability to make such ingenious nests wherein the spiritual seed of humankind would always be sheltered from predatory threat.

A keyword for the Woodpecker is progress, because she will doggedly hammer at her purpose until it bears fruit. Concepts of the determination and drive of this bird can also be understood when we consider the Woodpecker's love of the mighty Oak tree. Oak trees are symbolic of strength of character, endurance and stability.

The most nurturing of the Solar totem animals, woodpeckers are the consummate listeners, and are sympathetic and understanding. The woodpecker is the one to have on your side when you need support, and they will prove to be loyal and protective. They make wonderful parents, and equally impressive friends and lovers. Another feather in their cap is their amazing capacity for organisation, frugality and resourcefulness. The woodpecker has a tendency to be jealous, possessive, angry and spiteful, but can also be extremely caring, devoted and romantic in a supportive environment.

SPIRITUAL KEEPER ★ COYOTE

Your spiritual keeper guides your spiritual growth and brings illumination. Your spiritual keeper is determined by the season in which you were born. Regarded as the 'keepers' or 'caretakers' of the Universe, the four Directions or alignments were also referred to by the Native Americans as the Four Winds because their presence was *felt* rather than seen. The Direction to which your birth time belongs influences the nature of your inner senses. The South Direction's totem is the Coyote. The Coyote is a symbol of growth, fruition, emotions, productivity and fluidity. The Coyote is bold, impetuous, charming, youthful and creative, and as a spiritual keeper, can endow us with these qualities. In some native tribes, the Coyote is referred to as a trickster or joker. A clever, cunning and amazingly adaptable animal, its message is of wisdom and folly. Operating year-round, the Coyote doesn't try to trick us, but rather mirrors our own human capacity for stupidity and cleverness.

Challenging the status quo, the Coyote sometimes becomes unstuck but is ever the triumphant survivor. To the Indian, this animal is a creator, teacher and keeper of magic, and even when the magic does not work, it serves a purpose; the Coyote knows there is always hidden wisdom. Playful as well as skilful and agile, the Coyote teaches us not to take things too seriously, and that anything is possible if we understand that wisdom, balance, intellect and fun can all co-exist. Through this spiritual keeper, we can reawaken the child within, stimulate our intuition and open up the mind. Coyotes hunt in cooperative groups, in an organised fashion - while one chases, one will rest, then they switch - which can teach the value of teamwork. The howl of this animal is a social call, usually warning of danger or to bring attention to its loneliness, reminding us too of our own primal needs and connections. The Coyote's teachings can help you negotiate a difficult situation, and can highlight the traps we may be caught in, or ways we could be fooling ourselves. It is an especially powerful healer when it comes to relationships, because it is when we are in one that we often fool ourselves the most. Following the Coyote won't make you a fortune, but its lesson is to teach us that material wealth doesn't equate to true happiness anyway. Your animal keeper the Coyote is, above all, a potent symbol of the need for the balance between wisdom, trickery, skill, cleverness and cunning.

CLAN ★ FROG

Your clan animal comes from a place of inner knowing and intuition, helping you to discover the essence and magic of your true self. The Frog, a Totem of the Water clan, represents the song that calls the rain to Earth, and cleansing, teaching us the opportune times to purify, refresh and replenish our reserves. A charm or amulet in the shape of a frog is said to attract true friends and to help you find long-lasting love. To the Ancient Egyptians, Romans and Greeks, frogs symbolised inspiration, fertility, good luck and speedy recovery from illness, beliefs that carry over into some cultures today. People of the Frog clan have deep, easily flowing feelings, which enable them to have empathy for others and to heal. They have natural gifts for healing, sensitivity, creativity, and a deep appreciation for rain and being around water. Frog clan people are blessed with an abundance of emotions, feelings, perception, insights, and the ability to pick up on the innermost feelings of others. They are also able to delve into the incredible depths of the Soul. As the Moon is so strongly associated with emotional and watery realms, Frog clan people can connect with this deep Lunar magic by studying the cycles, patterns and energies of the Moon, the ruling celestial sphere of their clan animal, the Frog.

THE MOTH & CANCER

The moth is a presence of the night, like your Lunar ruler. Like butterflies, moths are primarily a symbol of reincarnation, transformation and regeneration, because of their ability to metamorphose from egg to caterpillar to moth. The concept of moths as souls in transit, especially those who die during the nocturnal hours, is found in a number of cultures including the Chinese and the Australian Aboriginal. The attraction of moths to the light is regarded as an attempt to make the transition to the spirit world. As a species that has existed for about 60 million years, the moth is therefore not surprisingly a symbol of immortality. Overall, metamorphosis is the essence of moth's magic: the egg stage is symbolic of the birth of an idea, the larvae stage represents the foundation, and the chrysalis stage is symbolic of the manifestation, and the growing of wings symbolises taking flight and exploring unchartered territories.

THE OWL & CANCER

★ Keywords ★
Wisdom, Knowledge, Help, Support, Revelation

The Owl is sometimes known as the Ancient Wisdom Keeper. The Owl has long been associated with the need to retreat from the world. Owl energy teaches us to look inside ourselves for the answers we seek. A powerful spirit guide when embarking upon meditation or study, the Owl will help you to keep secrets. The Owl is also linked with the night and Moon magic. This majestic bird is revered by other animals for its wisdom and knowledge and because it is mostly nocturnal and can see in the dark, is also linked with prophecy. The American Plains' Indians saw the Owl as a protector and ruler of the night, so wore Owl feathers in certain magical rituals to offer them protection. Athena, the goddess of wisdom, was given the Owl as her symbol and the bird has been associated with learning ever since. Owls can also be a symbol of evil or bad luck in some legends and cultures.

Though not all Owls are nocturnal, magically and mythologically they are creatures of the night. When they swoop, with wings outstretched and huge wide eyes, across the face of the Moon or pale against the darkness, they resemble ghosts, and indeed they are associated with spirits in numerous cultures.

The link between Owls and folklore is ancient. This bird was the symbol of ancient Athens, and the silver four-drachma coin bore the image of the Owl as a symbol of that city's patron, Athena, the Greek goddess of wisdom; hence the idea of Owls as messengers of wisdom. Athena's Roman counterpart Minerva also had the Owl as a symbol. In many other cultures, especially that of the Native North American, the Owl was a wise teacher of traditions. To the Celts the Owl and the Owl goddess were linked with the Moon. The Owl was the bird of the Crone, an association that was later transferred to banshees, especially in Scotland (a banshee might appear as an Owl flapping at the windows of the dying). This accords with the role of the Owl in warning of death, since an Owl heralded the deaths of the Roman emperors Julius Caesar, Commodus Aurelius, Agrippa and Augustus. Among the Maoris of New Zealand Owls are revered as guardian spirits of the community and wise ancestors. In the children's classic Winnie the Pooh, problems usually prompt Pooh to seek Owl for advice since, "If anyone knows anything about anything, it's Owl." It is the nocturnal habits of most Owl species that probably led to their being attributed with occult powers. This was highlighted by their noiseless flight, due to their velvety surface, their intense fixed gaze, and of course their superb night vision, the last which may be responsible for its connection with prophecy and its reputation for being all-seeing, clairaudient and clairvoyant.

Changeable, free, independent and as mutable as the wind, the Owl is a difficult one to pin down. With its easygoing nature and radiating a natural warmth, the Owl is a friend to the world. Notorious for engaging in life with a tank full of enthusiasm, the Owl whole-heartedly loves adventure and challenge. Although he or she can be reckless, careless and thoughtless, he or she is also very adaptable and versatile, making a great teacher, artist or conversationalist. The Owl can be excessive, over-indulgent, extravagant, tactless and belligerent, but in a nurturing, supportive environment, he or she will be an engaging, enthusiastic and attentive listener. The Owl brings the totem gifts of a sense of adventure, wisdom, intuition, keen observation and discretion. It shares the power energies of silence, versatility, meditation, hidden knowledge, inspiring challenges, and putting one's heart and soul into everything, and brings forth and teaches the magic of embracing all, optimism, night vision, oracle, clairaudience and expansion.

THE TURTLE, TORTOISE, SCARAB & CANCER

In ancient India and Greece, the sign of Cancer was represented by a turtle instead of a Crab. This may seem peculiar to us, but there are many similarities between the tortoise and the Crab. Both have hard shells and very soft interiors; both retreat into their shells when threatened; and both move at a slow but constant pace.

In ancient Babylon Cancer was represented by a tortoise, and by 2000 B.C. in Egypt it had become a scarab, a symbol of immortal life also associated with Leo. The scarab beetle was a sacred totem referring to the soul.

YOUR CORRESPONDING CHINESE ASTROLOGY ANIMAL

The Chinese Zodiac, known as Sheng Xiao (literally meaning 'birth likeness'), is based on a twelve-year cycle, each year in that cycle related to a particular animal. These animals are: Rat, Ox, Tiger, Rabbit, Dragon, Snake, Horse, Sheep, Monkey, Rooster, Dog and Pig. The selection and order of the animals that so influence people's lives, particularly in East Asian cultures, originated in the Han Dynasty (202 BC - 220 AD) and was based upon each animal's traits, characteristics, tendencies and living habits. Further, ancient people observed that there were twelve Full Moons in a year, and that, among other similarly related celestial observations, suggests its origins are also based on astronomical concepts.

The legend of the Chinese zodiac's story usually begins with the Jade Emperor, or Buddha (depending on who is telling the tale), summoning all the animals of the Universe for a race or a banquet. The twelve animals of the zodiac all appeared at the palace, and the order in which they arrived determined the order of the Chinese zodiac.

Each oriental animal corresponds with a Western astrology sign. For Cancer, it is the Sheep.

> "I am nature's special child.
> I trust and am rewarded by trust.
> Fortune smiles upon my countenance.
> All things blossom
> In the gentleness of my love.
> I strive to find beauty in all I behold.
> I am fair of face
> And full of grace.
> *I am the Sheep."*
> **Theodora Lau**

Chinese name for the Sheep ★ YANG
Ranking Order ★ Eighth
Hours ruled by the Sheep ★ 1 p.m. to 3. p.m.
Direction ★ South - Southwest
Season and principle month ★ Summer - July
Corresponds to the Western sign ★ Cancer

★ SHEEP ★ *Fixed Element Fire*

★ Keywords ★

Wise, artistic, elegant, gentle, compassionate, honest, genuine, inventive, impractical, sensitive, dependent, creative, pessimistic, materialistic

The Sheep is the eighth animal of the Chinese horoscope. Traditionally a yin sign, the Sheep is sometimes symbolised by a Goat. Typically, Sheep are timid, tasteful, altruistic, peaceful and calm. You can be easily led, however, and tend to become sulky if challenged. You need security and harmony to be at your best. A contemplative and retiring sign, you prefer to be in your own home or within your own group, living in peace and comfort. Creativity is one of your greatest gifts, and you can create an atmosphere of beauty, charm and fantasy with effortless ease. The catch with all these soft and fluffy characteristics is that they can frustrate or irritate more outgoing types. Your herd instinct is strong, so you usually live with others, but fail to do your share of the tasks, preferring to spend time on fun, dreamy, artistic or impractical pursuits. You are whimsical and good-natured overall, and although you lack foresight, when you really want something, you know how to get it.

YOUR METALS

Cancerian power metals are Silver and Aluminium.

Although the magic power of crystals is widely recognised and applied, the influence radiating from metals is often overlooked. Metal, too, emits a powerful energy and in fact, in Chinese philosophy, metal is considered so essential and powerful that it is classified as one of the elements, alongside Air, Fire, Earth and Water.

As already mentioned earlier in the book, throughout the writings of early philosophers and theorists, there are countless references to the unmistakable mystic connection between the seven known planets of the time, and Earthly affairs, ailments and objects. Seven metals were connected with the seven planets, to which seven colours and the seven 'transformations' were added. So the ancient alchemist came to share the astrological doctrine that each planet ruled a mineral: The Sun ruled gold, the Moon silver, Mars iron, Venus copper, Saturn lead, Jupiter tin, and Mercury quicksilver. Consequently, in alchemical symbolism the same sign came to represent the nominated metal and its corresponding planet.

SILVER

The chemical symbol for silver is Ag, which comes from its Latin name *argentum*, meaning 'white or 'shining'. More abundant than gold, silver has long been regarded as a precious metal, which has numerous applications beyond its use in coin currency. Silver is very ductile, durable and malleable, and apart from being suitable as a univalent coinage metal, it can be found in jewellery, ornaments, tableware, Solar panels, mirrors, stained glass, batteries, medicines, water filtration systems (it prevents algae and bacteria from building up in filters), and also in investments in the form of coins and bullions. Silver compounds are also used in disinfectants, catheters and other medical instruments. Natural silver will never rust, however since the industrial revolution there has been sufficient sulphur in the air to tarnish it.

Silver, like copper, is considered a purely positive metal, clean and incorruptible. No ill effects can come from wearing it, nor is any quantity considered unhealthy. Among the most popular materials for amulets, it is believed to provide a spiritually protective influence to one's aura and immediate environment. Associated with the goddesses Artemis and Diana, it is thought that wearing silver jewellery aids fertility and if you wish to start a family, charms are the most potent if carved from this metal.

Silver in its pure native form (elemental silver) is actually very rare, as it usually occurs mixed in ores with other metals. Most silver is produced as a by-product of gold, copper, zinc and lead refining. It is a soft, lustrous, white transition metal, possessing the highest electrical, thermal conductivity, and reflectivity of any metal.

Silver has been used for thousands of years for ornaments, adornments, utensils, trade and currency, and its value as a precious metal was long considered only second to gold. Regarded as one of the 'noble metals' along with gold, its desirable properties led to it being ascribed a variety of mystical and even supernatural powers.

Most of us associate silver with jewellery, however only a small amount of mined silver is made into coins, jewellery and utensils. The most common use of this metal is in photographic film *. When you take a photo, silver crystals are produced from the film emulsion. These crystals react to the light and capture the image.

The crescent Moon, the astrological symbol of your ruler, has also been used as the alchemical symbol to represent silver since ancient times, and the visual appeal of this metal is reminiscent of the silvery Lunar light it emits.

* The use of silver in photography is rapidly declining however, due to lower consumer demand with the advent of digital technology.

PLANTS, HERBS, SPICES, TREES, SHRUBS, FLOWERS, SCENTS & INCENSE

Plants have long been associated with magic, medicinal properties, superstition, nutrition and even astrology. In ancient times, some were endowed with magical properties based upon beliefs of the time, but also upon anecdotal evidence that some herbal concoctions, flowers or essences helped alleviate and even cure uncomfortable, painful or dis-eased physical or mental states. Whether these were based upon 'old wives' tales' or beliefs in supernatural forces matters little, for in modern times we can prove and indeed *have* proven through scientific research and controlled experiments, that plants have their place in our health and medicine cabinets. Some 'magical' plants have aphrodisiac or narcotic properties, while others have formidable toxic effects, but all are considered in some way to affect the human system on physical, spiritual and psychological levels. Plants such as cocoa, tobacco and coffee, which have accompanied humans over the course of millennia, are still, more than ever, an integral part of our daily lives. They still incite the same pleasures, the same fascinations, and the same dangers, and some still carry the same taboos. It is interesting to note that more than 80 per cent of chemical medicines in existence today, and found in pharmacists' dispensaries, are made from plants.

In modern astrology herbs are often associated with the zodiac signs and have evolved from an old system where a specific planet rules each herb. The planet that governs a herb is chosen according to its appearance, scent and where it grows; herbs are additionally categorised as hot or cold, and dry or moist. In this way you can see how the nature of the herb corresponds to the nature of the planet. If you are familiar with your ruling planets' basic associations, you will find it easy to match it to herbs. Although you can simply buy whatever herbs you wish to use for your magic, the optimum effect will be obtained if you can gather them at a favourable astrological time. Once you are armed with astrological knowledge, you can choose a time when the planet that rules your chosen herb is in a position of strength. Keep in mind that each planet rules a substantial amount of plants, so if one isn't easily obtained, it should be simply to find another one to use for the same purpose.

There sometimes seems to be a wide variance in the list of herbs associated with a specific astrological influence. This is because the different parts of the plant have different rulerships and uses. For example, whichever planet rules it, a plant that bears fruit is naturally related to Jupiter, its flowers relate to Venus, seed or bark to Mercury, leaves to the Moon, wood to Mars, and roots to Saturn. So, as well as the planet that traditionally rules the plant, it can be regarded as having a secondary ruler according to the part of the plant being used. Although you don't need to work with a highly complex system of deciding which herb will suit your purposes, you can make your magical workings more powerful by paying attention to some of these nuances.

Essentially, different scents, herbs, flowers and plants have their own specific vibrations. Their essences should be worn on your skin (you can make up your own combinations using essential oils or flower waters), burned in an oil burner, inhaled from a cloth, diffused in a bath or bowl of steam, or burned as incense sticks. Many plants, herbs and spices, however used, contain gentle yet effective energies which will affect not only your wishing ceremonies, but also your moods, associations and emotions, which can assist in carrying your wonderful Self in the direction of your dreams. Lifted up on incense smoke, for example, your wish is carried out to the wider Universe. Try making your own, out of any or all of your power plants, woods, flowers, shrubs, trees or herbs!

Thirty-three magical, mythical plants are: Cocoa, rosemary, tobacco, thyme, wheat, coffee, sugar cane, cinnamon, hemp, tea, pumpkin, foxglove, incense, amanita (a mushroom), tarragon, pepper, rice, belladonna, reed, ginseng, clove, ginger, sage, maize, mistletoe, lily, mandrake, St John's Wort, poppy, peyote, cinchona, verbena and the vine *. How many of your Cancerian 'lucky plants' (listed under the next sub-category, 'Your Lucky Plants, Herbs, Spices', etc.) can be found on this Magical 33 List?

YOUR LUCKY PLANTS, HERBS, SPICES, TREES, SHRUBS, FLOWERS, SCENTS, OILS & INCENSE

Honeysuckle, Larkspur, Iris, St John's Wort, Rosemary, Hyssop, Poppy Seeds, Salt, Ginseng, Anise, Ginger, Lemon Balm, Water Lily, Poppy, Butterbur, Polypody, White Rose, Willow, Acanthus, Sycamore, Lotus **, Chickweed, Ground Ivy, Marigold, Tarragon ^, Dog's Tooth Violet, Verbena, Sundew, Bog Bean, Peppermint, White Poppy, Spearmint, Hawthorn, Convolvulus, Alder, Saxifrage, Watercress, white flowers in general, and trees rich in sap. *

For the Moon ★ Waterlily, Lettuce, Poppy, Walnut, Silver Birch, Willow *

* Some plant products can be poisonous, toxic, hallucinogenic or even fatal if consumed. Always research first.

^ This herb has connections with your Lunar ruler. The French name for Tarragon is 'artemisia', from the Greek goddess of the Moon, Artemis.

** A Note on the Lotus Flower ★ The lotus flower - which has its roots in the mud but arises out of it beautiful and clean - is a symbol of how we can all rise, glorious and triumphant, from the muddiest of conditions. Indeed, Hindus and Buddhists consider the lotus an emblem of purity, as its beautiful flower comes from a plant that grows in slime. The Ancient Egyptians believed the goddess Isis was born from a lotus flower, and so they associated the lotus with fertility and sexual potency. The

Hindus believe the creator god Brahma was born from a golden lotus flower that was sighted in the navel of the Universe. And one legend about Buddha tells that everywhere he walked, he left lotuses behind him instead of footprints. The lotus holds a spiritual significance and meaning for many traditions. Across all, the lotus is a symbol of creation: out of the mud, the world can be born. It is also a symbol of wisdom, expressing the truth about the possibilities for all living things. The Buddhist mantra "Om mani Padme hum" translates as "Om, jewel in the lotus, amen." Reciting this mantra is said to bring peace to the chanter and to those nearby. A thousand-petalled lotus symbolises spiritual enlightenment.

YOUR SPECIAL POWER FLOWERS

CANCER IN GENERAL ★ Acanthus

OTHER BIRTH FLOWERS ★ White Rose, Convolvulus, Geranium & Water Lily

JUNE BORN ★ Rose ★ Love is the magnificent birth gift of the popular rose, with most representing aspects of love, affection or feeling - rosebuds signifying unawakened love, red roses deep emotions, white roses purity and innocence, yellow roses joy and friendship, pink roses gentle emotions and gratitude, orange roses passion and desire, and black roses death and farewells. The rose has always symbolised beauty, love and fertility. It was sacred to Aphrodite and Venus, the Greek and Roman goddesses of love. The Romans often planted roses on graves, as they regarded it as a symbol of rebirth. In Islam the rose is associated with paradise, and in the Christian tradition, the rose represents the Virgin Mary's purity and beauty. One ancient Christian legend says that until Adam and Eve were expelled from the Garden of Eden roses had no thorns; God added these to remind people that they no longer lived in a perfect world.

JULY BORN ★ Larkspur or Delphinium ★ Named for the irrepressible dolphin (from the Greek delphis), the blooming delphinium bestows health and a talent for happiness on those born in July.

YOUR FOODS

The Moon goddesses that rule Cancer symbolise sensual abundance and fertility. Think of these buzz words: glowing, sensuous, generous, dense, rich. Leave the calorie counting to others. Home and hearth, meadow and hayloft live at the sensual heart of Cancerian appetites. Warm them, sweeten them and always offer them an after dinner mint in front of the fire for extra comfort and pleasure. Motherly, devoted, affectionate and loving, the Cancerian just adores nurturing others and makes the most delightful cook and homemaker of the zodiac. Your kitchen is likely to be homely, comfortable, aromatic and soft, with a whole wall full of cookbooks, imagery and ornaments to complement its life-giving energy. Crabs love most cuisines, as all types of foods appeal to you, however you are not adventurous and are quite timid when trying new things; you would prefer to stick with the tried, tested and true. Your ruling planet the Moon rules the colour white, so creamy, rich, substantial foods are normally your flavour of the day. Loving of comfort and nourishment, you enjoy robust *and* delicate, hearty, sustaining pleasures of the plate and palate - and put much care and time into preparing all your meals. You adore dining out, being waited on by your loved one, and equally love waiting on others. The creamy, fleshy texture of oysters and other Lunar-ruled seafood such as caviar, crabs, prawns and clams are all enjoyable to you. Overall, the more tender loving care, time and patience are put into making the dish, the more appealing you will find it! Slow-cooked, nourishing, warming and home-style were made for the Cancerian palate. Fast, poorly presented, exotic and adventurous are definitely not on the menu for the Crab.

CANCER POWER FOODS

"Let food be your medicine; let medicine be your food."
Hippocrates

Succulent and Fragrant Foods appeal to the Cancerian palate, as do Seafood (especially shellfish), Caviar, Seaweed and Kelp, Cheeses, Cream, Milk, Yoghurts, Figs, Chocolate, Pale Vegetables with a High Water Content (Cucumber, Cauliflower, Lettuce, Squashes, Celery, Cabbage), Papaya, Nuts and Citrus Fruits. Your power beverages are White Wine, Milk, Spring Water, Hot Chocolate and Miso Soup. *

* Caution: Always use essential oils, alcohol and/or herbs with caution and research each one prior to use, as not all are safe for use by certain people, or under certain conditions such as pregnancy, intoxication or illness. Some herbs and oils may be hallucinogenic, toxic in high doses, or produce other undesirable effects, and may be considered potentially harmful or hazardous if used or consumed before operating machinery, driving, or combined with alcohol or other drugs. Always consult a qualified practitioner or undertake thorough research from reliable sources before use or consumption of any of the listed essential oils, herbs or foods.

YOUR LUCKY WOOD ★ BIRCH
(Great to make a magic wand out of!)

Native Americans referred to trees as 'Standing People' because they stand firm, obtaining strength from their connection with the Earth. They therefore teach us the importance of being grounded, while at the same time listening to, and reaching towards, our higher aspirations. In Norse mythology, Yggdrasil, the tree of life, is a cosmic map that represents all life. The tree has its roots in the Underworld, is linked to the Earth through its trunk and its branches reach into the air of the Otherworld of spirit. The dryad, or tree's spirit, needs to be respected and asked when 'taking' from a tree for the purposes of magic. The essence of tree magic lies in understanding the qualities of each type. These can be drawn on for such things as healing and spell-casting. For example, the rowan tree grows high up the sides of mountains, often in hard-to-reach places, so if you need to develop tenacity or access to difficult spiritual spaces, you can call on this tree; the oak tree is durable and strong, so if you are needing fortification or firmness, you can gain power from this tree. When respected as living, breathing beings, trees can provide insights into the workings of Nature, cycles, and our own inner essence. Each birth time is associated with a particular kind of tree, the basic qualities of which complement the nature of those born during that time. Appreciate the beauty of your affinity tree and study its nature carefully, for it has a connection with your own nature and lessons to impart.

BIRCH ★ The word birch comes from the Sanskrit root *bharg^*, which means 'shining', for the areas in which it grows contain snow which melts and sends cascades of water down its trunk, the birch bark taking on an appearance of liquid glitter. When it rains, the bark becomes so wet and dark, it is named the black birch. Birch carries properties of protection, exorcism, healing and purification.

The medicine of the cherry birch lies in its inner bark, which contains a rich, fragrant oil known commercially as wintergreen. The name wintergreen hints at the birch's effectiveness as a transitional plant between winter and spring. Spiritually, the black birch assists us in locating within our own bodies the signs of spring which have been buried under winter's cold, barren landscape and its oil assists us in shedding our protective winter layer to make way for our fresh 'green' selves to sprout.

The cherry birch thrives when it grows near water, giving us a signature of its gift as a tonic to the Watery elements and needs of the human body. In Russian tradition, birch trees were deeply revered through song and story. But while eastern European folklore focuses on the protective powers of birches, the Nordic countries consider birch the symbol of the Earth Mother, embodying the female, cyclical powers of growth and healing. Traditionally, witches' brooms are made of birch twigs, twine and wood, so if you feel drawn to witchcraft and the feminine aspects of magic and spirit, then birch wood might be a wise choice for you.

The immense durability of birch bark has been put to many uses; from Native American canoes and ropes to writing parchment. Using birch bark as a medium for the written word strengthens your connection to the tree's claim of being a 'tree of knowledge' and a gateway to new ideas and worlds. The tough substance of this bark indeed survives long after the original tree has died. Although strong, it is easy to work with.

In western Europe, the beautiful and graceful birch is referred to as the 'Lady of the Woods', belonging to the element of Water and under the dominion of the planet Venus. It is believed that if one wishes to communicate with the goddess, one should sit silently in a grove of birches and listen for her whispers, which travel on the gentle wisps of wind.

Throughout its life cycle, the birch continues to be both a useful and versatile resource. As a pioneer tree, it gives way to other larger trees, sacrificing itself to make way for new life. It is therefore associated with the circle of life, endings and beginnings, and new growth.

The birch tree is the Celtic tree of beginnings, an association springing from the fact that it is the first tree to grow back after a forest fire. The birch also sheds its bark, which suggests further links with renewal, as the old and worn-out is released to make way for the new. Creating and carrying a staff or wand made out of white birch wood is an ancient, wise way of allying one's self with qualities of communication, truth, perception and clearer vision. Wands can be fashioned and used to point the way to clear intent and fresh beginnings in life, or a kind of rebirthing of the soul.

The silver birch tree has special associations with the Moon as, interestingly, its bark reflects the moonlight, making the tree appear to glow in the light of a Full Moon.

YOUR SACRED CELTIC CALENDAR TREES
★ OAK OR HOLLY

OAK ★ (10 June - 7 July)
HOLLY ★ (8 July - 4 August)

The Celts and other ancient peoples had many beliefs and traditions based around the magical lore of trees. The system of Celtic tree astrology was developed out of a natural connection with the Druids' knowledge of Earth cycles and their reverence for the sacred knowledge they believed was held by trees. The Druids had a profound connection with trees and regarded them as vessels of infinite wisdom. Their calendar, being based on a Lunar year of thirteen months, contains a tree for each of these Lunar months, corresponding with (but not exactly) each of the twelve western astrology zodiac signs, which are based on the Solar calendar. Because there are some crossovers, I have included two possible trees for your zodiacal birth period.

OAK ★ Oak wood corresponds to the element of Water and the planets Jupiter and Mars, and is a symbol of strength, sovereignty, courage, wisdom, wealth, honesty, toughness, endurance, rulership, nobility, generosity, justice, protection, bravery and power. With its towering height and wide girth, it also symbolises and bestows luck, vigour, love, potency, health and prosperity. The mighty oak tree has a wide trunk, very deep roots and deeply lobed leaves. The older a tree, the larger it will be and mature trees can be well over 1,000 years old (their life span is up to 2,000 years). Held sacred in ancient times, its noble attributes have long been harnessed for use in magic, and today the oak is still valued for its great strength and durability.

Oak is known as the 'King of Trees' and has a strong association with English woodlands, which has its origins in Britain's Pagan past. It is connected with the Summer Solstice; its wood being used to fuel the sacred Midsummer fires. It also has links with royalty and kingship: King Arthur's round table was fabled to have been created from a single cross section of a large oak. In the 'old days', front doors were usually made from oak; this was because, although the thickness of the wood helped to keep the warmth in and unsavoury guests out, its magical properties also provided strength, fertility and protection to the house or building. The word 'druid' originates from the Celtic word 'duir', meaning 'oak' or 'door'. It was believed that the oak was a portal to the spirit world and nature gods were worshipped in oak tree groves.

Acorn nuts, the Divine fruit of the mighty oak, are said to increase fertility, sexual potency, longevity, 'immortality' and youthfulness, fostering virility partly through the sensuality of their creamy texture and smoky flavour, as well as the protein richness they offer. Both nut and cone have been used magically in fertility charms. Acorns are also omens of wealth, happiness and extremely good fortune. The acorn and the tree from which it comes, is a portent which signifies successful outcomes to any venture you want to undertake, and prosperity and growth in the future.

Furthermore, the oak tree's essence helps boost energy levels and to achieve our goals and manifest our desires. Oak is a grounding wood, offering the gifts of stability and strength; imbued with the tree's powerful properties, it can be used to make magical tools or charms. The power and durability of the oak tree are demonstrated by the fact its root system extends as far beneath the Earth as its branches stretch above it. Its strength is further symbolised by enduring what others around it cannot; it remains strong through challenges, and is regarded as being almost immortal, as is often attested by its long life and ability to survive fire, lightning strikes and other similar devastations. Oak is one of the most sacred trees, traditionally prized by the Celts and Druids, the tree's commanding presence signifying true alignment of purpose, balance and fortitude, and Witches often danced beneath the oak tree during ritual. Carrying any part of the oak tree draws good luck to you, but remember first to ask for permission and above all, to show recognition and gratitude for this wood's amazing gifts.

Oak types are the great stabilisers and protectors of the Celtic tree system. You are gifted with a strong, nurturing, generous and helpful spirit, and a voice for the underdog. You are the 'gentle giant' crusader who exudes an easy confidence and naturally assumes everything will always work out well. Having a deep respect for history and ancestry, you love to impart your knowledge of the past to others. You need structure and control over your life, and a large family setting suits you best, ensuring a long, happy and full life.

HOLLY ★ Holly is traditionally associated with Christmas, and is used to decorate homes at Winter Solstice. Its red berries and green leaves in the dead of (northern hemisphere) winter symbolise everlasting life. Holly carries properties of exorcism, healing and purification. With its protective qualities, a holly tree grown near the home is thought to provide protection from thunder, lightning and demons. A masculine tree, the prickly leaves of the holly match its formidable associations as a tree of protection and warfare, and its wood was used to make spears and chariot wheels in ancient times.

The holly is a sacred tree of the Sun and is associated with the Sun god in Wiccan beliefs. The roots of this belief lie in the tree's hardy, evergreen qualities and its connection to the Winter Solstice, as the shortest day of the year symbolises the rebirth of the Sun, and the Wheel of the Year now turns towards the summer. Evergreens have a special significance with the Winter Solstice: they represent the undying light of the Solar influence as they retain their leaves all year.

The fine, hard wood of this tree is especially good for carving and inlay work, and its wood, berries, leaves and flowers, can be used in many spells, magical tools and charms. Its best known use is the tradition originating from the medieval practice of hanging a 'Holy Bough' made from holly and other evergreens, in the entrance of homes at Christmas, to welcome guests. This gesture also symbolised goodwill and longevity.

Holly carries a regal status in Celtic tree astrology. High-minded and noble, those born during the holly period are said to have no issues taking on roles of leadership and power. You take on challenges with ease, overcoming them with vigilance, skill and tact, meaning you are seldom defeated. You are competitive, ambitious and confident, which may make you come across as arrogant, but under the façade you are generous, kind and affectionate. But because many things come to you so easily, you have a tendency to rest on your laurels and can become lazy and complacent.

ESPECIALLY FOR AUSTRALIANS
(OF ALL ZODIAC SIGNS)

If you live in Australia, here are two Australian-based magical woods, for those who prefer to source their woods closer to home and nature. Australia has a less documented history than many European civilisations, but still has no less mythology and legends swirling in its mists of time.

EUCALYPTUS ★ Eucalyptus is very plentiful and has a wonderfully intoxicating, distinctive, clean aroma which is reminiscent of the continent's vast areas of bushland, and has played an important ceremonial and medicinal role in the culture of Australian Aborigines, who have inhabited the nation for 40,000 to 50,000 years. Eucalyptus is a wood of feminine energy whose elemental association is Earth and main origin is Australia. One of the strongest healing woods known, eucalyptus wood has been used for centuries for medicinal as well as ritualistic purposes. Heady and Earthy, the energy of this wood is clean and pure. Eucalyptus is recommended for the promotion of good, robust health, and is also related to luck, especially if regarding knowledge. An excellent tool in divination, particularly when worn as a charm to invoke luck, it brings the wearer or user good fortune when used in rituals seeking positive results.

LEOPARDWOOD (or LACEWOOD) ★
Leopardwood or the Leopard Tree, so named because of its spotted wood, carries the energies of both the masculine and the feminine, Mars (Aries, Scorpio) and Venus (Taurus, Libra), and its main affinity is with the Water element (Cancer, Scorpio, Pisces). Leopardwood is a very useful tool for divination and is associated with positive luck, earning it the label 'gambler's wood'. Overall, its energy is very positive, making it an ideal wood for use in almost any ritual or spell, especially those concerning luck, magic and divination.

THE POWER OF LOVE

Each Sun sign exudes their own love and romance style. This style is an energy unique to that sign, and has the power to magnetise to that person their true, soulful match. Unhappy or unsuccessful relationships are often the result of incompatible Sun signs, personal values, goals, hopes, viewpoints or expectations. I believe everyone has a perfect soul partner (or three!) who is especially for them, and just knowing that special person or persons are out there can illuminate your life's romantic path. In this lifetime, we may not find that person or persons, but can still experience the joys and wonders of many other significant relationships which enrich and add tremendous meaning to our lives. Some partnerships are only fleeting, but the feelings they give us can last a lifetime, while others are more enduring, and the rewards they give us and lessons they teach us can last a lifetime too. Small gestures of love on a frequent basis, consistent nurturing and communication, and making the effort to understand each other, are just four ways to keep the fires of passion and romance burning long after the initially roaring fire has diminished into glowing embers.

Your whole natal chart would need to be examined to form an overall picture of your romantic nature, and although the Sun is a fantastic starting point, it is not the sole consideration. Regarding these other planets, in Carl Jung's studies on psychological astrology, and in traditional synastry (the comparing of two people's natal charts to determine overall compatibility), the harmonious link between the Sun in one person's chart and the Moon in the other's (usually the man's Sun and the woman's Moon) is considered the best indication for a happy and enduring relationship. More specifically, the sextile aspect, an angle of 60 degrees, appeared most frequently between the Sun of one and the Moon of the other in fulfilling relationships. Other positive planetary contacts, such as one person's Moon to another's Venus, or the Mars to the Moon (again, traditional indications of attraction and harmony) also occurred frequently.

The feminine personal planets in a male's chart (Moon and Venus), and the masculine personal planets in a female's chart (Sun and Mars) tell a lot about the inner self and how this is projected onto relationships. However helpful chart analysis is in telling a story about your relationship style and approach, it all depends not on your chart, but on what you do with the resources at your disposal, which your chart can indeed tell you a lot about. Relationships and marriages involving harmonious planetary and zodiacal energies between the two people tend to last longer because they are simply more 'flowing' and easier.

The signs in which the four personal and 'relationship' planets - the Sun, the Moon, Venus and Mars - are placed, coupled with the aspects they make with the other planets in the chart, give important clues into understanding the often unconscious drives within you that shape your relating style, tastes, mannerisms and patterns.

Expanding upon the other planetary considerations is beyond the scope of this book, but it is useful to know, particularly if you are interested in examining the dynamics of a current relationship a bit deeper, or are wishing to attract a new one into your life. But for now, your Sun sign is a wonderful place to start! Your Solar sign is regarded as being at the core of the complex - and very fun - study of relationships! So for now, we will begin this study of love with your essence, your core self, the brightest light shining from within - your Sun sign!

SOME LUCKY-IN-LOVE TIPS
GENERAL HINTS

★ To attract and retain love, the Heart chakra (an energy centre within the body) needs to be balanced and clear from blockages. The Heart chakra is located in the region of the physical heart. Its Sanskrit name is *anahata*, and its symbol is a twelve-petal green lotus flower whose centre contains a green circle and two intersecting triangles making up a six-pointed star representing balance (and also could be said to symbolise six as the number of Venus). Its element is Air and its colour is green. Balance in this chakra is expressed as unconditional love for ourselves and others. Crystals that can be used to cleanse and balance this chakra are mostly green and pink stones.

★ Pink candles (two, representing a couple, or six, representing Venus, is preferable) can be used in love spells.

★ Any 'love-attracting' wishing rituals should be done on a Friday (ruled by Venus) night around the time of the New Moon (signifying the principle of increase and growth).

★ Basil, otherwise known as witch's herb or St Joseph's wort, is said to be the most potent lover herb of all. Basil vibrates to the energy of Mars, which is all about lust and sexual energy, and it is used prolifically in all sorts of love potions and rituals throughout the world.

★ Ginger has a reputation as a potent sexual tonic and aphrodisiac *. Arousing and warm, it can increase sensual vitality, particularly in men. Being warming and spicy, its vibration aligns with Mars. Saffron is also regarded as a potent, albeit expensive, aphrodisiac!

★ Wear red and pink (associated with Mars and Venus respectively), as these colours in all their shades are said to incite passion, lust and romance. Green is also connected with the heart by virtue of its association with the Heart chakra and the planet Venus, and its links with fertility, nature, abundance of all kinds, and new growth.

★ Call upon some higher spiritual help. When working your 'love magic', some planetary influences, goddesses and gods that you can call upon are: Aphrodite, Venus and Eros/Cupid, and other lesser known deities such as Juno Lucina, Demeter, Freya, Ishtar, Circe and Hathor.

★ The planet Venus has developed a rich culture of gods and goddesses associated with her varying levels of love and passion. These include the virgin - Brighid; the fertile woman - Aphrodite, (the Greek goddess); and of course Venus (the Roman equivalent); the mother and provider - Demeter; and desirous or physical love - Eros/Cupid (Venus's son).

★ The pine tree is sacred to Adonis (Venus's lover) and is said to balance the male and female energies. Pine is cleansing and protective and, as an evergreen, symbolises life. Its cones represent fertility.

★ Cardamom is said to have aphrodisiac qualities.

★ The three almost universally recognised symbols of love are the goddesses Venus and Aphrodite, and the Cupid. Venus is the patroness of flowers and vegetation, and represents the regenerative cycle of creation, as well as beauty, herbs and physical love. She can be called upon for general love wishes and rituals. The dove, roses, rings, copper, apples, rosemary and the ankh are some of her sacred symbols. Aphrodite is a Greek goddess who has the ability to bring lovers together. Her names means 'of the sea' as she is believed to have been born of the foam of the ocean. She can be called upon in ceremonies and spells for affection, love, marriage and partnership. Some of her associated symbols are the Flower of Aphrodite, swans, dolphins, frankincense and myrrh. Cupid, the cherubic winged boy with a bow and arrow, is the Roman name, and Eros is the Greek name for the same deity. The son of Venus/Aphrodite, he is an aspect that represents lustful love and desire.

★ Heartsease, another name for the wild pansy, Latin viola tricolour, was one of the most popular additives to the love potions of the ancient Romans and Greeks.

★ In centuries past, when people were more in tune with nature and its cycles, ceremonies, rituals and festivals were held on certain dates or times of year. The following are some examples, and you can reawaken their powers through craft and ceremony: February 2 is Bridhid's Day, or Bride's Day, and represents the white goddess; February 14 is Valentine's Day, traditionally the greatest and most well-known love 'celebration' of the year; March 1 is one of the festival days of Juno Lucina, the light bearer and goddess of women and marriage; the month of April is especially linked to the love goddess Aphrodite; the Summer solstice which falls on or around June 21 is an important time for reconnecting with the spirit of love, fertility and marriage; August 1 is the first of three harvest festivals in the Celtic calendar: The Harvest Festival honours Demeter, the goddess of love, as bountiful mother and faithful wife; the Festival of Lights, Diwali, in October, is sacred to Lakshmi, the Hindu goddess of happiness, love, and good fortune; the Winter solstice which falls on or around December 21, marks the turning point from long dark nights to lengthening days, and is the time of the wheel of love when virgin goddesses gave birth to their children - it is also fittingly symbolised by evergreens such as pine, ivy and holly; in Mexico, December 31, the last night of the year, is traditionally 'wishing night' and is an opportune time to make a wish for a lover in the coming year, using evergreen branches to enhance your request.

* The term 'aphrodisiac' is derived from Aphrodite, the Greek goddess of love, beauty, lust and sensuality

★ GEMSTONES ★

When it comes to calling love into your life using crystals, the general rule is that any of the pink or green stones are closely aligned with matters of the heart and can therefore help you to entice the affections you seek. Although your Sun sign has its very own special gemstones, outlined elsewhere in the book, the following stones can be used by all the signs (except for the first point, which are your own sign's feature stones), as their energies and qualities contain the power to attract and create love in all its forms, from self-love to deeper soulful connections with another, or to increase states of being which open the heart, thus enhancing your abilities to magnetise love.

★ Moonstone, Pearl and Ruby ★ Using your Cancerian luckiest crystals is a fabulous start to working on heightening your romantic zest, and making your sensual energy more potent. Emerald is also useful in raising your attracting powers.

★ Rose Quartz is the ultimate love stone. It invites love into your life by helping to open your heart to receive love, and gently reminding you that you are worthy of love. Connected with the Heart chakra, it is the stone of unconditional love, enhancing all forms of it and opening up the heart. It is excellent for increasing self-worth and acceptance. The colour of rose quartz is pink, the colour of Venus, the amorous planet of desire and nurturance. Balancing and calming, it helps to heal emotional pain. Wear this stone, keep some beside your bed, or sleep with some under your pillow to remind you that love it coming your way - and that you whole*heart*edly deserve it!

★ Green Aventurine is considered the 'opportunity and luck stone'. Connected with the Heart chakra, it helps us to recognise opportunities and is said to place us exactly where we need to be for good things to transpire, as energetically it opens our mind and heart to increased perception to recognise lucky elements. It also promotes new growth, optimism, and is an overall attractor of good fortune, adventure and abundance.

★ Jade, on a spiritual level, has an affinity with the Heart chakra. It harmonises relationships, and encourages compassion and the establishment of strong bonds.

★ Emerald is reputedly a stone of constancy in love, and is said to have been brought to Earth from the planet Venus. Because it is green, it also holds deep associations with the Heart chakra.

★ Rhodochrosite can be used to attract one's soul mate. This stone, as with all the pink stones, can be used as an effective love magnet. It encourages you to appreciate yourself by teaching you that you are worthy of love, wholeness and happiness - and so opening you up to receive.

★ Malachite, Citrine, Rhodonite, Moonstone, Morganite, Beryl, Ruby, Mangano Calcite, Garnet, Red and Pink Tourmaline, Tugtupite, Rutilated Quartz, Lodestone, Peridot and Lapis Lazuli are also known for their love properties, and can be used or worn to invite romance into your life, or to bring and retain enduring love.

★ Clear Quartz can be used with any of these listed crystals to amplify their metaphysical properties.

★ Shells: Although shells are not technically a crystal, but rather a natural elemental material, they are associated with love and are sacred to Aphrodite, the Greek love goddess, and are often used in magic talismans to attract romance.

★ ESSENTIAL OILS ★

The following essential oils are known for their aphrodisiac or love-attracting properties also, and can be worn as perfumes on the skin, used in an oil burner or vaporiser, dispersed in a bath, used in spell-casting and wishing rituals, sprinkled on your pillow to imbue your dreams with inspired romantic notions, or in any other creative ways you can think of! **

★ Essential oils, flowers and herbs which contain natural pheromones or like substances, or increase pheromone levels in the body, are: Lavender, Frankincense, Jasmine, Nutmeg, Ylang Ylang, Sandalwood, Patchouli and Asian Agarwood (Oud).

★ The prime love oil, which holds Universal appeal, is rose. Reputedly excellent for both the mind and body, roses are the basis of more than 95 per cent of women's fragrances, and the petals have a long tradition of uplifting the spirits and soothing the soul. *Rosa damascena* is believed to be good for attracting love, while *R. centifolia*, the French rose oil base, is regarded as an aphrodisiac. Rose is traditionally accepted as the all-encompassing Universal fragrance of love, blessed with a reputation for opening up the hearts of all those who come under its spell.

★ Cedarwood oil has been used since ancient times in incense and perfumes. Its deep, woody scent helps to stimulate the Base chakra, increasing sexual passion and desire. Its sedative qualities aid relaxation and encourage openness. In herbal magic, it is also associated with spells for wealth and abundance.

★ Neroli, Geranium, Almond (as a base), Basil, Thyme, Vetiver, Gardenia, Vanilla, Rose Otto, Apple, Cardamom, Lotus, Orange, Ginger, Bergamot, Rosewood and Clary Sage are also exquisitely seductive and sensual, and can be used in any way you like to bring to you that which your heart desires. These oils, when mixed with your own pheromones and magical intentions, will naturally enhance your point of attraction!

** Always research first and use with caution.

CANCER ★ LOVE STYLE

To Cancer, love is tender and sentimental. In a true Cancerian, love has a lot to do with security, for yours is the most sensitive and security-seeking of all the zodiac signs, especially in romance. You are self-sacrificing and responsive to your partner's needs, as well as being devoted and faithful almost to a fault. You are vulnerable and rarely show your feelings openly, so you may mask your emotions, be fearful of rejection and afraid to trust readily, but once you feel secure in a relationship, your love is deep, sentimental, generous and intensely loyal. You love to be adored, cherished and comforted; and you love to adore, cherish and comfort in return. Nobody gives cuddles, affection and love like a Cancer whose heart has been opened. Kindness and sympathy are never in short supply when you are involved in a relationship, and although you are capable of intense passion, you are quite discriminating about where and with whom that passion is expressed. You are also considerably slow to commit this passion, because trust is so innately vital to you and this often takes a while to build. Cautious and slow to 'allow someone in', you hide yourself under many layers before you will slowly begin to peel them off and bare your soul and your moods. Indeed, if your loved one can decipher your moods, then he or she is in with an excellent chance of winning your hard-won heart. It shouldn't take too long to interpret that sullenness means you feel rejected; clinginess means you need assurance; possessiveness means you need a deeper commitment; going silent means you are afraid; whining means self-pity; crabbiness means you're feeling unappreciated; and on and on it goes, like the ebbs and flows of the tides and the Moon cycles. In fact, your moods and feelings are so pervasive that you often don't know where one ends and a new one begins. Overall however, Cancer's loyalty is inextricably linked to your need for security - which provides the basis for *all* your relationships and without which you will seek it elsewhere. But in any case, no separation is ever easy on your delicate, sensitive soul, even if you deeply long for freedom. After all, attachment and sheltered love to you are as essential as your element Water is to life.

LUCKY IN LOVE? CANCER ★ COMPATIBILITY

* Please note the following is based on your Sun sign alone. For a whole and integrated approach to relationship compatibility, your whole natal chart would need to be taken into consideration. Synastry (*syn*: acting or considered together, united; *astry*: pertaining to the stars) is a branch of astrology which delves into more complex areas, and is based upon the natal charts of the two people concerned, to determine overall compatibility, potential conflicts and suitability based upon celestial influences. For the purposes of length, the below information is simplified and only refers to Sun sign connections.

Cancer ★ Aries * ♋ ♈

The Ram's tactless and impetuous nature may hurt or confuse the sensitive Crab. Cancer admires the Aries's dash and courage, but unless the Ram is more careful and empathetic, the Crab may very well scuttle away and hide. Aries is bold and direct, the Cancerian is timider and more private, yet your Cardinal natures can combine to make a potentially powerful coupling here; your enterprising and shrewd characters help you sniff out opportunities and develop them together with initiative. Your ruling planets, Mars and the Moon, exercise two very different energies in the relationship. The Crab may prove too emotional and clingy for the adventurous, independent and impulsive Aries, and Cancer may find Aries's careless attitudes difficult to handle, unsettling, and perhaps even hurtful to their touchy nature. Cancer is home-loving while Aries feels stifled when domestically 'caged in'; Cancer has a protective, security-seeking nature whose interests lie primarily in their homes, children and families, while Aries will happily circulate amongst anyone indiscriminately. Overall, the Ram may inadvertently upset the Crab's dedicate feelings, and the Crab will react with passive resistance through retreat or worse, sulking and bottling her emotions inside. If Aries can muster up enough patience and emotional empathy to cope with this fragile and moody character, this relationship stands a chance of working. Otherwise, over time, the Water may indeed put the Fire out.

Overall compatibility rating ★ 5.5 out of 10
Lucky Romance Tip ★ To attract an Aries, wear the colours red or orange, and use the crystal diamond

Cancer ★ Taurus ♋ ♉

With Taurus's Earthy love of home and Cancer's Watery love of home, you two can definitely tango, but are both inclined to be clingy and possessive in your own different ways. Just bear in mind that Earth and Water can also create mud! But generally speaking, there is a natural affinity between your elements, so you will have more in common than not. The Cancerian will no doubt make the Taurean heart beat a little faster, in the most tender way possible. You both love comfort, security, warmth and protection, and your solid base is a very pronounced sense of family and home life. Feelings, emotions and affections are of paramount importance to both of you, and Taurus appreciates the attention, sustenance, nurturing and care which Cancer so enjoys giving. Taurus, who lives her life according to her senses, is a born epicure, and this will be compatible with the Cancerian's love of food - somehow the Bull instinctively knows that the way to Cancer's heart is through the stomach. Being basically conservative, cautious and conventional, conflicts and clashes are unlikely, however the Crab's strong emotions and moods could make the normally unshakable Bull feel a little unsettled at times. This should be a fairly easy and effortless union, for both of you can create a very comfortable and sharing environment, and although different in many ways, your differences are complementary rather than divisive, so you make each other feel safe and supported. The Bull will just need to be ultra-sensitive to avoid crushing the Crab's shell.

Overall compatibility rating ★ 8.5 out of 10
Lucky Romance Tip ★ To attract a Taurus, wear the colours pink or green, and use the crystal rose quartz

Cancer ★ Gemini ♋ ♊

Cancer's sentimentality and over-emotionality may make Gemini feel uneasy and may not evoke a deep response in him, as Gemini has little time for fathoming the Crab's deep feelings and incessant moodiness. Overall, these two have very different aims. Gemini loves to talk, but will not necessarily have the sensitivity to Cancer's feelings to say the right things, making it hard to build up trust. The Twins are so busy doing things, that the Crab may often feel neglected. Any sulking that ensues will not be tolerated by the freedom-seeking, mentally-oriented Twins. Gemini wants excitement, while Cancer craves domestic security. If Gemini can curb his restless streak, the Cancerian may trust him with her tender heart and happiness. Cancer's slushy emotions can seem self-indulgent and even petty to Gemini, yet this nurturing Water sign can be just what the Twins need to settle their highly strung nerves. The Crab may prove too emotional and clingy for the footloose and fancy-free Twins, and Cancer will find Gemini's pressing need to be a social butterfly dizzying, and perhaps even hurtful to their highly sensitive nature. Cancer is private while Gemini shares with everyone; Watery Cancer is emotional while Airy Gemini is intellectual; Cancer is home-loving while Gemini feels stifled when domestically 'caged in'; Cancer seeks sentimental love and a meeting of the hearts, while Gemini seeks friendship and a meeting of the minds. Gemini's fickle and changeable nature may unsettle the soft-hearted Cancerian, whose protective, security-seeking nature means her interests lie primarily in home, hearth, children and family.

Overall compatibility rating ★ 5 out of 10
Lucky Romance Tip ★ To attract a Gemini, wear the colours light blue or yellow, and use the crystal citrine

Cancer ★ Cancer ♋ ♋

This pairing has all the right elements for a match made in Watery heaven. Both emotionally-charged Water signs, Cardinal and ruled by the Moon, you might very well wrap yourselves up in each other's embrace and live happily ever after there. In any case, two Crabs will produce a relationship in which feelings, emotions and soft and fuzzy sentiments reign supreme. If you agree, this combination will bring great happiness, nourishment and security, but the reverse can also occur. You could become so entangled in each other's emotional turmoil that you forget there is an outside world. Cancerians also tend to keep a lot hidden and are private to a fault, so penetrating the underlying depths of the other's fluid worlds may take a lot of guesswork, and result in frustration and communication breakdowns. On the whole though, if your feelings flow as they should and you get along in most departments, there should be no such difficulties in understanding each other - in fact, you are almost telepathic in your empathy and understanding of the other. But remember that this can have its drawbacks, as so much insight into each other's psyches may prove draining, overwhelming or create tensions. Overall, you are both Lunar-ruled, sympathetic, nurturing, loving, security-seeking and tenacious, so this will help in any times of trouble. Emotions can make clear thinking a challenge, so beware not to become hurt or muddled by each other's often misconstrued actions or needs.

Overall compatibility rating ★ 7.5 out of 10

Lucky Romance Tip ★ To attract a Cancerian, wear the colours silver or white, and use the crystal moonstone

Cancer ★ Leo * ♋ ♌

As the 'father' and 'mother' of the zodiac, your Fire and Water combination has the potential to be a good one. However, Cancer may be a little clingy and needy for the more extroverted Lion's spirit. But although Cancer's Water is not compatible with Leo's Fire, your rulers the Moon and the Sun *do* complement each other, so despite your very different natures there is a chance here for a strong bond. The Crab will often have to give way to the dominant Lion, but the latter has the qualities which make Cancer's Moon shine brighter. Moreover, Leo needs the adoration, attention and praise which the Cancerian is more than happy to give, and Cancer will certainly never wish to take the shine off Leo's limelight. Leo can create drama, and Cancer will patiently nurture her Lion through these outbursts. But Cancer will have to impose limits on how much energy she gives to the Leo's persistent need for theatrics, as it can be draining to the Crab's sensitive psyche. Also, the Lion is known to roar, rant, rave and boldly state his opinion, which could trample the Cancerian's delicate feelings and leave her feeling hurt. However sensitive Cancer is, she always knows exactly what she wants and the Leo will admire her for this - as long as she doesn't outshine him. He will also adore the Cancerian's cooking and knack of keeping house, for he loves beauty, comfort and a secure environment almost as much as she does. In any case, these two will likely take turns in playing the emotional dramatist in the relationship, but they have vastly different styles of expressing their innermost feelings: The Lion will roar, while the Crab will sulk. Leo likes to bear responsibility, and Cancer will appreciate his chivalry, generosity, affection and warmth. Around the Cancerian, the Lion may very well dull his roar to a loud, contented purr - after all, he is a soft fluffy kitten at heart, and Cancer will bring out his best in this regard. If Cancer's over-sentimentality and emphasis on emotions doesn't weigh the relationship down too strongly, these two could make much fun - and an epic love story - together, because, as this duo demonstrates, Water sometimes makes the Fire positively sizzle!

Overall compatibility rating ★ 7 out of 10
Lucky Romance Tip ★ To attract a Leo, wear the colours gold or orange, and use the crystal ruby

Cancer ★ Virgo ♋ ♍

Cancer's creativity and caring ways may turn Virgo on, however the Crab's emotional dramas and tendency to hoard, whine and cling clashes with Virgo's need for logic, reason and simplicity.

Your two elements Water and Earth blend well together, but the Virgo's incessant nit picking and thoughtless criticism may wear down Cancer's much more fragile feelings. The Virgin is intellect-based and the Crab is emotion-based, so you could be at odds with each other. If the Cancer can learn to cope with the Virgo's naturally cool and aloof façade, you have the potential to make this partnership work, as you are both sensuous, caring, compassionate and devoted. In return for the Virgo's imparting more order and system to the Cancerian's life, the Crab will coax the Virgin out of her emotional reserve and provide a few much-needed lessons in feeling, affection, romance and contentment. Cancer is hyper-sensitive and easily hurt, so the Virgo may need to curb her tendency to criticise and analyse every last detail. Virgo's tendency to be undemonstrative may also upset the needy Crab, who needs hugs, attention and security, while Virgo may lose patience with Cancer's proneness to sulking and moodiness. Both of you are also likely to be anxious and prone to worry some of the time, and you could both become melancholic and unreachable to each other should one or both of you go through a bout of depression. Overall, this is a strong pairing with fair potential, if the Crab can learn to live with the fussy, cool Virgo's pedantry and need for perfection.

Overall compatibility rating ★ 7 out of 10
Lucky Romance Tip ★ To attract a Virgo, wear the colours white or yellow, and use the crystal sapphire

Cancer ★ Libra ♋ ♎

This challenging combination of Libra's Air and Cancer's Water can seem a bit staid for the rather detached, Airy Libran. When the Crab tries to cling onto Libra with her firm pincers, Libra will tend to wriggle free with all his might. However, although

Water and Air are generally not very compatible, your rulers the Moon and Venus vibrate to a harmonious energy and give this relationship a warm, cosy feeling. Both peace-loving, affectionate and giving, there is good potential here. Cancer is easily hurt but unless Libra is provoked he is unlikely to do or say anything to cause any conflict in the union. If trouble does arise, both of you would sooner scuttle off than confront the other, but both in your different ways of course - Libra's way is denial, avoidance and evasiveness, Cancer's simply to hide away until the storm passes. Also, the normally balanced Libran would never do anything to upset the Scales or cause the relationship to get out of kilter. Cancer's natural desire to love and protect will be appreciated by Libra, however if it spills over into clinginess the Airy, rather more detached Scales will feel put out. Another point of difference is that Libra is intellectually-based and Cancer is emotions-based, which could cause rifts, as Libra strikes a fine balance between reason and emotion, so may be unsettled by Cancer's excess of feelings. The Crab's childish sulking will also not be tolerated by the more sophisticated Libran, and Cancer will want deeper levels than the more superficial Libra is willing to open up to her. Libra also pays too much attention to outward appearances, which could dishearten Cancer. Overall though, you are both romantic and loving, so if you can build a bridge over any differences and get over them, this could be a heavenly and enchanting pairing.

Overall compatibility rating ★ 7.5 out of 10

Lucky Romance Tip ★ To attract a Libran, wear the colours pink and blue, and use the crystal opal

Cancer ★ Scorpio ♋ ♏

Two Water signs can build a cosy nest. Cancer's emotional tactics are an open book to Scorpio and sometimes Scorpio likes to shock the Crab into noticing them. You are both hidden by nature but usually bring out the best of each other when you do come to the surface to share. You two share the Watery element, making your relationship comparable to a towering, powerful cascade of passion and love. Scorpio is intensely emotional and naturally possessive, and although her intensity may be a little daunting to the Crab's much more delicate expression, there is much common ground here. Facts, logic and reason will rarely feature in this pairing, as you are both ruled primarily by feelings and the inner depths. When harmony reigns, this is a very constructive duo, but if conflicts arise, emotions can get out of control and clear thinking becomes distorted. This also has the potential to be an extreme and complex match: you will either drown each other or swim along merrily together, keeping each other buoyed in the roughest of oceans. Although the Crab is clingy and possessive, the Scorpio's controlling, powerful nature may overwhelm her at times, but she can just as easily be swept off her feet by the suave and magnetic Scorpion. Whether your relationship survives or not will depend upon other factors of the two people involved, but however it turns out in the end, it will be an affair to remember - Scorpio doesn't do anything by halves and Cancer never forgets. Both of you seek security and faithfulness from your partner, so there will be an unspoken agreement here. Each of you is intuitive and can always sense what is going on, so mutual trust is essential here. Cancer, although delicate, has a way of understanding that Scorpio can sometimes be ruthless and tough. Great heights, depths and achievements are highly possible in this relationship.

Overall compatibility rating ★ 9 out of 10
Lucky Romance Tip ★ To attract a Scorpio, wear the colours red or burgundy, and use the crystal malachite

Cancer ★ Sagittarius * ♋ ♐

This is not an easy combination - the Crab is totally unlike the Archer in both personality and style. The Sagittarian may initially find the Crab mysterious and magnetic, but needs to beware of their tendency to cling or to hide, and their passive-aggressive tendencies. However, charming, chivalrous Sagittarius should have no troubles winning over the soft, tender heart of the impressionable and easily-swept-off-her-feet Crab. But although there may be an undeniable initial attraction between you, the relationship potential here is relatively low. The adventurous Archer is far too wayward and freedom-seeking to be domesticated by the home-loving Cancer. Cancer seeks security, while Sagittarius seeks freedom; Cancer loves staying home in comfort, while Sagittarius thrives on adventure and change; Cancer is private and hidden, while Sagittarius is sociable and extroverted; Cancer is clingy and co-dependent, while Sagittarius loathes being tied down or restricted in any way. Sagittarius's natural flirtatiousness will inevitably hurt the Crab's delicate feelings, and Cancer is often far too emotional for the much more mentally-oriented Archer. Security-seeking Cancer may not find her home in the Sagittarius's arms, as he is non-committal and flighty, ever in search of new, expanded horizons. The Archer will not tolerate the Crab's sulky moodiness, as he is an eternal optimist and has little time for reflection or brooding. You might give this partnership a good shot, as you both love affection and play, but an unbridgeable gulf may develop as you ultimately speak very different languages and exude vastly differing ways of expressing them. But at the very least you both have big hearts and the faith that love can indeed conquer all.

Overall compatibility rating ★ 6 out of 10
Lucky Romance Tip ★ To attract a Sagittarius, wear the colour deep purple or royal blue, and use the crystal zircon

Cancer ★ Capricorn ♋ ♑

You and your natural astrological opposite have a lot in common - and also a lot to teach and learn from each other. Cancer's sentimental, dependent nature will either melt Capricorn's heart and bring out the Crab's protective instincts, or make Cancer turn cold and suspicious. This is a generally harmonious combination of opposite temperaments, which could result in real success. If you apportion your roles wisely, you will certainly have the basis for a happy home environment. However, because you are zodiacal opposites, this partnership could be both complementary *and* competitive. If the Goat gives top priority to ambition and success, the sensitive Crab may feel left out, hurt or neglected. Cancer needs assurance, sentiment, warmth and constant care, which Capricorn often withholds for whatever reasons. However, the Crab will appreciate the security, stability and consistency that the Goat can ultimately provide in spades, and both are deeply sensual and introverted, meaning you will share many nights curled up on the couch and be quite content with this arrangement. Overall, Capricorn is a conditional lover when the circumstances call for it, which may unsettle the unconditional, devoted Cancerian, who gives her all to her loved ones. As well, the sometimes cold Capricorn is too icy for the warmth-seeking Cancer, and Capricorn may not understand the Crab's moods and sulkiness. The Goat's spirit is more independent than the Crab's clingy nature will tolerate, and Capricorn's discipline, guardedness, and emotional self-restraint will not serve to coax Cancer out of her reserve. If you can work through your polarities and reach a middle ground, this relationship has fair potential and good odds of enduring.

Overall compatibility rating ★ 7 out of 10

Lucky Romance Tip ★ To attract a Capricorn, wear the colours brown or black, and use the crystal garnet

Cancer ★ Aquarius ♋ ♒

Your ruling planets, the Moon and Uranus, will exercise two very different energies in your relationship. Further, your elements Air and Water, and your modes Fixed and Cardinal, don't blend easily. The Crab will prove too emotional and clingy for the intellectually-inclined, freedom-seeking Aquarius, and Cancer will find Aquarius's naturally cool and aloof nature unsettling, and perhaps even hurtful to their highly sensitive nature. Cancer is private while Aquarius loves to share; Cancer is personal while Aquarius is impersonal; Cancer is home-loving while Aquarius feels stifled when domestically 'caged in'; Cancer seeks sentimental love and a meeting of the hearts, while Aquarius seeks friendship and a meeting of the minds. Overall, Aquarius is a Universal rather than a personal lover, who likes to share interests and ideas with friends and humanity, and Cancer has a protective, security-seeking nature whose interests lie primarily in her home, children and family life.

Overall compatibility rating ★ 5 out of 10
Lucky Romance Tip ★ To attract an Aquarian, wear the colours electric blue or turquoise, and use the crystal aquamarine

Cancer ★ Pisces ♋ ♓

This combination unites two Water signs, and since the Water element is related to feelings, emotions and intuition, these will always take priority over logic and reason in your relationship. As a result, some of the more practical considerations of life will often be neglected, muddled or confused. But if you can both reside in your Watery realms quite happily, this pairing should bring much romantic fulfilment, caring, understanding and sharing. You are both sentimental and feel things very deeply, and there is potential for great intimacy and a meeting of the hearts here. You are also very romantic, with a strong need to love and be loved. Difficulties may only arise when the Cancerian, being naturally possessive and clingy, feels abandoned by the Pisces's innate need for solitude, indulging in fanciful whims and solo astral travel from time to time. One thing is guaranteed however: no matter how often the Fish retreats into her own Watery depths, she will always eventually swim 'home' to find the loving her nurturing Crab waiting faithfully with a home-cooked meal and a warm embrace.

Overall compatibility rating ★ 9 out of 10
Lucky Romance Tip ★ To attract a Pisces, wear the colours mauve or sea green, and use the crystal amethyst

* With all Fire and Water combinations (i.e. Cancer with Aries, Leo or Sagittarius), it is easy to see how and why fire and water are natural enemies. Water can quickly put a fire out, and fire can dry up water. Fire usually works quickly, and water gently. In alchemy and astrology, both are important, and both must be carefully manipulated and controlled to make full effective use of their powerful, albeit vastly differing, natures. Fire can be brought back to a steady heat, whereas the pressure and force of water can be increased vigorously or to circulate more actively. As warm and watery beings, the human body demonstrates the miracle of fire and water combined. Water connects, flows and lubricates, and brings healing, its passive, gentle nature soothing away the scorching harshness of fire. One ancient text offers a mystical view of how water and fire are intertwined in the body, and suggests that it is through consciously combining these two elements that we can transform our inner state. Fire can initiate and inspire this quest for self-transformation, but once the fire burns down, life can be restored anew by water. Natural enemies? Mostly. Astrological passion? Absolutely!

YOUR TAROT CARDS ★ FOR LUCK, MAGIC, ENERGY, ABUNDANCE, QUESTING & MEANING

THE CHARIOT & THE HIGH PRIESTESS

Tarot and astrology are inextricably linked. All the cards of the Major Arcana, which comprises 22 of the Tarot's 78 cards, are 'ruled by' or connected with either one of the twelve zodiac signs, the planets and luminaries, or one of the four elements.

The 22 Major Arcana cards contain the richest symbolism of all the cards in the Tarot deck, each carrying a myriad of messages for the reader to decipher. The symbolism contained within these images represents the archetypal aspects of your character. It also describes the path your soul takes through each stage of life, revealing clues through which you can explore different parts of yourself. Each of the cards also represents an aspect of Universal human experience and has a name that either directly conveys the meaning of the card, such as Strength or Justice, or depicts individuals that represent these human archetypes, such as the Hermit or the Empress. The illustrations on each card contain one or more figures and tuning into a card's imagery enables you to grasp its meaning intuitively. Consider the demeanour of the characters, whether it is day or night, the background, any symbols, the buildings, the colours, the vegetation, the weather and the season. Every card has its own story to impart, and through entering that story you can gain deeper insights into the full picture of your journey so far, as well as illuminating your path ahead.

I have outlined two cards here for your sign: The Chariot and the High Priestess, which have links to your zodiac sign itself Cancer, your ruler the Moon, and your element of Water. These cards will have special meaning for your sign, and can carry powerful messages and lessons for you to reflect upon.

★ THE CHARIOT ★
Ruled by Cancer

Keywords ★ Victory, Willpower, Control

★ KEY THEMES ★
Triumph Over Difficulties ★ Struggles and Battles ★ The Arrival of Help at the Hour of Need ★ Positive and Fruitful Efforts ★ A Journey ★ Good News ★ Expansion ★ Control Regained ★ Progress Success ★ Audacity ★ Faith ★ Fighting Spirit ★ Positive Outcome ★ Beneficial Change ★ An Important Achievement ★ Self-Discipline ★ A Great Leap Forward ★ Positive Challenges ★ Willpower ★ Public Recognition ★ Perseverance ★ A Promotion or Award ★ Travel Modes of Transportation ★ Willpower

Number ★ 7
Astrological Signs ★ Cancer & Sagittarius

THE MESSAGE ★ Carrying the spoils of war, a princely warrior triumphantly wins the race. With a robust physique and stern resolve, the Chariot driver has harnessed not only his considerable energies, but also those of nature. Self-assurance and bravado have held him in good stead in the headlong race against formidable opposition. By suppressing feeling and emotion, the Chariot driver has held onto the reins and moved from barren fields into green and flowering ones. The Chariot indicates a man who combines imagination with mental discipline and tenacity, displaying natural leadership abilities.

THE STORY ★ Here a victorious young man, standing upright in a chariot that has four columns and a luxuriant canopy, sets out on an adventure, or returns triumphant from battle. His chariot is drawn by two horses or sphinxes, who offer him wisdom, but may also represent his sexual drive and spirituality. He is powerful, demonstrated by his crown, and he is positive in outlook. The Chariot is representative of achievement, popularity, control and celebration. You may feel that your particular chariot is being drawn by two very different horses because doubt, uncertainty, struggles and conflicts plague your journey. However, the outcome will be worthwhile. The Chariot is also a card of movement, travel and transport.

THE AWAKENING ★ The ability to relate to another increases your sense of inner strength and guidance, allowing you to make decisions to consciously initiate changes in your life. In order to triumph, you must take the reins of control and not let go. Enlist the help of outside forces in your quest, and know that right now there is no time or place for emotions, just single-minded concentration on your goal. This need for control shifts into the knowledge that by being focused and true to your objectives, you can shape the course of your life rather than drift along aimlessly. You are quite right to feel strong and optimistic, and should accept any challenge that is offered. The Chariot encourages you to expand your horizons through study and adventure, for whatever your age you are young at heart! You can now focus your will and work towards your goals. The time is ripe for travel, intellectual journeys and fulfilling your potential. The qualities that have enabled the Chariot driver to succeed, however, carry a word of warning: you must enjoy this moment of glory with the knowledge that it, like other such moments and heroes, will pass. It is vital not to become so flushed with success as to become arrogant.

THE LESSON ★ The Chariot announces a situation to come, in which one has to move forward, show courage, willpower and determination, and feel confident in order to attain one's goal. It represents conflict, but a necessary one - one that encourages change and growth. It is the force of destiny which drives one to achieve great things. The Chariot indicates overcoming snares and obstacles, with the help and protection of Providence. The Chariot is an encouragement to go forward with the choices that have been made, and the objectives that have been set. It is also a strong sign that you will gain victory, and sometimes foretells a move, travel, movement in general, a journey or a piece of unexpected good news that you are about to receive. Be self-reliant and you will gain success.

SYMBOLISM *★ The Chariot represents the power of the will over the body, emotions and mind. In essence, it signifies one's ability to exercise control when deciding on a new course or direction, as the mind and emotions can be fickle and easily influenced. The Chariot symbolises success and marks a new stage or change in circumstances. It denotes a certain degree of detachment, as it illustrates how we can be affected by the senses and yet still manage to conquer them and forge ahead.

The Chariot shows three-fold imagery - the Chariot driver, detached and powerful, and the dual forces of the two horses that he drives and controls. The driver appears confident, using the force of his will to guide the Chariot's movement.

The two horses or sphinxes drawing the vehicle represent the opposing tides of the mind and emotions that would gallop out of control and cause confusion if not ruled by a greater force - the indomitable will.

The chariot depicted on the card is sometimes drawn by two sphinxes, symbolising the mystery of the future as well as the positive and negative forces that persist through our lives. In Jungian terms, the Chariot represents the struggle between light and shadow. The sphinx also represents enigmas. Another image that appears frequently is that of two horses pulling or looking in opposite directions. Both images symbolise a struggle between two forces, both of which are strong and valid, but opposite in their desires. Usually, one of the horses is black and the other is white, further suggesting this apparent conflict and their opposing natures, and it is the task of the charioteer to keep those forces under control. In some cards where the chariot is being driven by two horses, one horse is aiming right, with its head turned slightly in that direction, while the other horse is going straight ahead, as if it were wearing blinkers or refusing any change of direction.

The number of the Chariot, seven, is usually considered a sacred, mystical number, embodying a sense of spirituality, accomplishment, magic, music and enchantment. And indeed, perhaps it is these which the Charioteer has achieved mastery over. It almost always symbolic of a victory of self-discipline, or the mind having achieved control over opposing forces, the theme of The Chariot being the balancing of opposites. Indeed, the balancing and integrating of differing forces is a common issue that appears in many cards of the Major Arcana.

The Charioteer is not necessarily cut off from his emotions, but he is not focused on them at this time; they may even be seen as 'entanglement'. He tells you that if you don't distract yourself with feelings but keep control of your reins and your eyes on the prize, whatever your goal, this focus will pay off. This should be a time when you are maintaining a strong division between your professional life and your feelings, but you have the ability to bridge the gap and connect the two if the task calls for it. In any case, you can harness the energies you need to accomplish your goal, just as the horses or sphinxes are harnessed and moving ahead.

The Chariot ultimately suggests an inner conflict, and the fact that the charioteer is clearly having trouble keeping his horses in control is an indication that his feelings are in opposition; he knows he needs to steer the middle course, but that isn't an easy task. This may translate into something simple, for instance one part of you wants to remain idle while the other half wants to undertake and complete a task, leading to an internal battle which sometimes has the outcome that neither side achieves a satisfactory result.

Although The Chariot suggests a state of inner conflict, it also indicates unexpected good news is on its way. Its other divinatory meanings are adversity, possibly already overcome, conflicting influences, turmoil, success, vengeance, the possibility of a voyage or journey, escape, rushing into a decision, the need to pay attention to details, and urgency to gain control of one's emotions. This card is about victory and conquest over difficult odds, the force of destiny which drives one to achieve great things, renewed optimism and motivation; by being self-reliant one can attain high levels of success.

Cancerians are recommended to carry one of these cards with them to illumine their paths, and to magnetise that for which they are asking. Go forth and claim the magic which is yours by using the symbolism of the Chariot as your guide!

★ THE HIGH PRIESTESS ★
Ruled by the Moon & the Element of Water

Keywords ★ Intuition, Wisdom, Knowledge

★ KEY THEMES ★
Desire for Esoteric Understanding ★ Seeking to Uncover Mysteries and Secrets ★ Mystical Powers ★ Dreams ★ Psychic Abilities ★ Unconscious Mind ★ Reliance on Instincts ★ Patience ★ Inner Calm ★ Guided by Intuition ★ Careful Consideration before Action ★ Knowledge that is Both Inborn and Acquired Experience ★ Wisdom ★ Forethought ★ Purity of Intent ★ Thoughtful Reflection Secret Knowledge

Number ★ 2
Astrological Signs ★ Cancer, Scorpio, Pisces & Virgo

THE MESSAGE ★ The High Priestess is the Seer who tunes into everything happening anywhere, anytime. She represents dreaming consciousness, latent psychic abilities, and the modes of perception many modern cultures have scorned, to their detriment and suffering. She embodies the highest spiritual values, representing an open door to the sacred realms of mysticism and magic. The High Priestess is telling you to learn from emotional situations. The answers you seek lie in your emotions and feelings, so trust your intuition and the power of your natural psychic abilities. Also, by paying special attention to your dreams and any intuitive messages you receive, you will be accurately guided by them. When she appears in a reading it means your intuition is functioning more strongly than your intellect. A wisdom is activated in you that is older and deeper than your ordinary mode of thinking. She signifies decision-making with an awareness of the hidden and the visible aspects of the situation. Stay open to your emotions and your feelings in order to come into contact with what you already know. Study spiritual topics, and remember that silence is golden.

THE STORY ★ The High Priestess is a private, all-seeing and spiritual woman with hidden depths and a deep compassion for others. Passive and quiet, she represents a vessel of memory and holy female wisdom. Her powers are so great that they are almost beyond actions, her timeless secrets communicated through an inner voice, and only those wise enough to retreat into silence and undertake thoughtful study will know them. The crown the High Priestess wears as headdress, is reminiscent of the waxing and waning Moon and the natural rhythms of the feminine cycle. These crescent horns of fertility connect her to the Lunar cycle - the waxing Moon forms one horn, the waning its opposite. It doesn't seem to be mere coincidence that the Greek word *delphi* is linked to the word 'uterus' and connects the High Priestess (and women) with prophecy, insights, divination and oracles. She effortlessly directs her psychic abilities in harmony with the desires of the Universe that is her child.

THE LESSON ★ The High Priestess imparts a simple yet meaningful message: Look for the answers to questions within your heart. Trust your insights, intuition and gut feelings, and act on your hunches. As she also represents learning, she indicates you should undertake a period of study - either formal, or that which comes about through your experience of life. It can suggest the start of training in the Tarot, clairvoyance, astrology, and other mystical studies which rely on intuitive application or psychic insight. She may also represent unnoticed 'power behind the throne', which indicates hidden influences at work and secrets to be revealed later. Something may not be currently known to you and you are not in possession of all the facts, so she advises that you wait until these are more fully uncovered to you before making any further moves. She could also indicate a female teacher or mentor will enter your life soon, or that you yourself will have some knowledge and wisdom to share with and teach to others. If you are in the process of trying to answer an important question about your life, the High Priestess invites you to relax and listen to your inner voice. Take a deep breath, and imagine an open, illuminated space in the centre of your chest where all wisdom resides, and let the answer come to you.

SYMBOLISM ★ The High Priestess sits between two pillars representing severity and mercy. Her robes are patterned with pomegranates, suggesting the mystery and richness of life and death. Her robe, her posture, the scroll she holds in her hand, and her crown, symbolise intuition and the ability to listen to, and act upon, inner authority and guidance. Symbolising all that is subtle and 'hidden', she holds the keys to the mysteries of life. She carries the knowledge of occult wisdom, which is accessed through her connection with the deep emotional self, and whereas the Magician in the preceding card manifests his power in more tangible ways and using physical tools, the High Priestess contains the power within *herself*, using her abilities for spiritual growth rather than outward expressions of her forces, and uses only her mind and feelings to achieve this.

The staff she grasps appears to connect both the heavens and the Earth, and symbolises that the High Priestess is the gateway to the conscious mind through the subconscious. She is able to access both spiritual and Earthly mysteries.

The peacock pictured in some cards symbolises the High Priestess's ability to choose to display her beauty, or to keep it hidden from view.

Silent, secretive, clairvoyant and enlightened, the High Priestess can guide us through the dark wood of ignorance, indicating that reason alone cannot guide us. Her task is to show us the way to the inner world of the collective unconscious. She has a book of wisdom on her lap, with its most esoteric secrets hidden under the edge of her cloak; behind her is the veil between the inner and outer worlds, or the spiritual and the material planes. And although we, as travellers on the Tarot journey, may not yet be ready to part this veil, we are being shown it exists. Her overall appearance is a message to go quietly within yourself to become aware of your eternal connection to All That Is, and the strength you gain from this knowledge will bring insight.

Depicted as a regal-looking young lady sitting between two pillars, which represent opposing forces such as life and death, The High Priestess acts between them. She has always had a spiritual meaning, and in older decks was known as the Female Pope or The Papess. She rules the shadowy world of the unconscious mind and imagination, and symbolises the creative process of gestation; indeed, the foetus must remain in the womb until it is ripe to birth itself, and nothing should be done to precipitate this moment. The lady shown on the card often wears virginal white, signifying unfulfilled potential. In some decks she appears holding a pomegranate, the many-seeded fruit of fertility, suggesting promise for the future. The High Priestess is connected with the Crescent Moon, which symbolises a new cycle of creativity, and she has links with Persephone, goddess of the underworld, and the Egyptian Lunar goddess Isis (in some cards the High Priestess is depicted wearing the horned crown of Isis).

This card can be a challenging card to interpret because of its hidden, elusive and shadowy quality. Her links with the underworld and the unconscious can suggest that she doesn't reveal her secrets easily. Despite its lack of apparent clarity, its divinatory meanings can be perceived as wisdom, sound judgement, serenity, common sense, penetration, foresight, objectivity, perception, intuition, self-reliance, emotionlessness, and platonic relationships.

The High Priestess compels you to withdraw from the chaos and noise of daily life and seek counsel from your guides and angels. Some secrets need to be decoded first, in order to be deciphered. In this way, the High Priestess has a lock, but she also provides the key to those who seek it. Meanwhile, know that everything you need to know will be revealed in time; you just need to foster patience and be led by your inner wisdom.

Know that the High Priestess only exists to help you and respond to your every question. While galaxies swirl above you, pose your query without any attachment to the answer you will receive. In time she will take her hands from behind her back, and in them will be the symbol of your answer.

* Please note that the images described are not found in all Tarot decks. The images in different decks can differ considerably.

THE TAROT'S SUIT OF CUPS ★ REPRESENTING THE WATER ELEMENT

The Cups correspond with the Water element and are an especially interesting and meaningful metaphor. Water is life-enhancing and sustaining when it flows freely; but if trapped or contained for too long, it becomes stagnant, blocked and unhealthy. And, like our emotions and feelings, water can change shape to fit any channel or container, as well as being able to transform into other forms, such as ice or steam. The Tarot Cups reveal the flow of our emotions, how turbulent or calm our inner seas are, how we express ourselves, and how this all influences the relationships we have with others. Their narrative tells the tale of our inner life and reveals hidden feelings. The symbol of the Cup resembles a chalice or sacred drinking vessel and brings to mind the Holy Grail or the cup of life. Consequently, the issues the Cups raise have a spiritual quality. The Cups are connected with the unconscious, artistic abilities, fantasy, feelings, attachments, intuition, love, pleasure, emotions, harmony, sensitivity, fertility, happiness and unity. The decorative imagery and themes that run through the suit of Cups are fish, mermaids and of course water. The fish is a symbol of creative imagination, and the element of Water represents the feelings and the depths of the unconscious mind. The Cups deal with the emotional level of consciousness and are associated with connections, expressions and relationships. The Cups suit can indicate that we are being ruled by our hearts rather than our heads, our emotions rather than our intellects, and therefore they may reflect instinctive responses and habitual reactions to situations.

The Cups are also linked to romanticism, fantasy, imagination and creativity. The Suit of Cups connects us to the wellspring of the spiritual source, helping us to develop our emotions and intuitive faculties, and to understand how we attract particular energies, relationships, experiences and events into our lives. The negative aspect of this suit include being overly emotional, relying too much on one's feelings, becoming disengaged or dispassionate, fantasising, idealising, and holding unrealistic expectations of ourselves or of others. All of these may manifest as repressed emotions, an inability to properly express ourselves, or a lack of creativity, self-confidence, faith or self-belief. In a deck of playing cards, the Cups correspond to the suit of Hearts.

THE LUCKY 13 ★ CANCERIAN TIPS FOR INCREASED MAGIC, LUCK & MAGNETISM

1 ★ Incorporate all manner of Cancerian symbols into your daily life to remind yourself of your soul's mission.

2 ★ Use the crystal Moonstone in any form in your daily life - wear it, meditate with it, hold it and carry it with you everywhere! Moonstone has a gentle nature, promotes kindness and peace, and is calming, balancing, soothing, healing, protective and uplifting, particularly to Lunar-inspired Crabs. This crystal opens the mind to hoping and wishing, inspiration and impulse, magic and enchantment, synchronicity and serendipity, and grants intuitive recognition and flashes of insight, allowing one to absorb what is needed from the Universe. It can assist to raise those emotions or states of being that assist in attracting wonderful things to you.

3 ★ Wear or surround yourself with the colours white, silver and pastel shades.

4 ★ Learn the way of the Goat by learning practical application, focus, determination, self-improvement and ambition. Capricorn has much to teach the Cancerian soul. Come gently down to Earth … Climb a little higher than you feel comfortable with … Work harder … Cultivate experience and wisdom … Become better with age … Feel the wonders of the Earth under your feet ... Enjoy the sensual feasts and fruits of your journey ... Celebrate your professional achievements ... Sit on top of the mountain and look out over the horizon; feel the wonder of the land below's vastness ... it's *all* within you!

5 ★ Use your lucky numbers 2 and 8, whenever you are needing an extra stroke of luck.

6 ★ Magnify and celebrate your compassionate and caring nature, your empathy with others, your amazing home- and family-building skills, your imagination, inherent spirituality and your intuitively in-touch psyche.

7 ★ Remind yourself of your mission constantly, that is by speaking, breathing and *truly living* your dreams and insights - give them form beyond your often hidden imagination!

8 ★ Focus your energies on exploring your inner depths, and transforming yourself through your higher psychic faculties - which are strongly accessible to the acutely feeling, receptive and sensitive Cancerian mind. Connect with your deep yearnings and inborn creativity through any means possible.

9 ★ Use your innate powers of emotional awareness, pure belief and metaphysical attunement to visualise and draw that which you desire towards you. If you can develop simple faith in the positive outcome of events, you can easily use your in-built intuition to great creative effect.

10 ★ Tap into and utilise your ability to guide, heal, empathise with, and transform others through sharing your emotions, spirit and soul. But to do that, you'll need to ease yourself gently out of your shell and onto the plane of existence where the rest of us reside! We need you out here with us at least some of the time!

11 ★ View your gentle, sympathetic nature as a strength and call forth the powers of your gifted, unique self. Be who you *really* are, without reservation or apology, and the rest will fall into place.

12 ★ Become the 'Nourishing Enlightener' of others - and yourself - that you were born to be!

13 ★ Once you have mastered greater self-confidence and allowed your soft inner self to come out and shine, learn to share the resulting abundance, insights and knowledge with others so they too can walk the Higher Path!

HAVE YOU PACKED YOUR MAGICAL BAG FOR THE JOURNEY?

If you wish to increase and draw more luck, love and abundance into your life, a power pack is essential. For Cancerians, I would recommend carrying or wearing the following items on you on your travels. Then just sit back and watch as magic pours into your experiences and realities, both inner and outer!

★ One of each of the following gemstones: Pearl, Moonstone, Ruby, Emerald.
★ Tarot cards The Chariot and The High Priestess.
★ A woodpecker in any form (use your imagination!)
★ Something made of silver.
★ An anchor symbol in any form.
★ A postcard or image from a watery, cool, rainy or oceanic place (representing your Phlegmatic disposition). Bon Voyage!
★ A postcard from the future to yourself, proclaiming, 'Wish You Were Here!'

A FINAL WORD ★ TAPPING INTO THE MAGIC OF CANCER

There is something inherently magical about Cancer, the deeply feeling hard-shelled, soft-centred Crab. Blessed with a gentle, feeling, instinctive and changeable nature, you are the caring nurturer of the zodiac. Nothing is harsh about you. The cosmos has endowed you with the precious and important gifts of tenacity, sensitivity, absorption, understanding, and an enchanting vulnerability. You are highly psychic, emotional and intuitive because you are the Chosen One who is open to the influx of Universal forces that channel themselves into your mind through the filter of the Lunar experience that is so unique to the Cancerian soul. Whether you are fully cognisant of it or not, a magical reservoir of energy is available to you to tap into whenever it is needed.

Finally, to attune yourself to luck, harmony and success, Cancerians should wear, eat, inhale, meditate upon, create, design, and dance with any or all of the suggested luck-enhancers for your Sun sign to receive the most beneficial astral vibrations these 'boosters' can offer you. Wearing, decorating and working with the amazing powers of all your lucky guides, animals, crystals, colours, woods, cards, herbs, foods, places, talismans, planetary influences, charms, numbers, and other magical tips contained within the words of this very book, will bring you greater abundance, love, magic, energy, happiness and personal power, and attract all manner of things to you like bees to sweet flowers. This, my Cancerian friends, I promise you - and Aquarians *never* lie.

Good luck on the rest of your amazing life journey, and may LUCK always smile upon you!

Lani is also available for personal Astrology, Numerology, Aura * & Tarot reading consultations, via post, email, Skype and in-person. Please email lalana76@bigpond.com for more information.

In-person only

Facebook Page ★ Astrology Magic

Other Books in the **Lucky Astrology** Series

Lucky Astrology ★ Aries
Lucky Astrology ★ Taurus
Lucky Astrology ★ Gemini
Lucky Astrology ★ Leo
Lucky Astrology ★ Virgo
Lucky Astrology ★ Libra
Lucky Astrology ★ Scorpio
Lucky Astrology ★ Sagittarius
Lucky Astrology ★ Capricorn
Lucky Astrology ★ Aquarius
Lucky Astrology ★ Pisces

Order your copies now, from White Light Publishing House, at www.whitelightpublishingau.com

www.ingramcontent.com/pod-product-compliance
Lightning Source LLC
Chambersburg PA
CBHW071155300426
44113CB00009B/1214